2 nodes Cluster RAC 19c
Installation and configuration
English Version

19ᶜ ORACLE®
Database

Erik Jourdain

Acknowledgments

Special thanks go to Darl Kuhn. His different books, for me a real reference. His time spent rereading me, his judicious remarks and his indulgence towards my poor command of English.

Erik Jourdain

Table of contents

Before reading

Some scripts in this book are available for download. Basic Virtual Machines are also availables for download.

http://files.silverlake.space

Index of /

Name	Last modified	Size	Description
adrci_fct	2020-04-03 10:55	1.4K	
cluster_alpha.pdf	2020-04-03 17:06	43K	
createYODA.sh	2020-04-03 10:53	6.4K	
db19c.rsp	2020-04-03 10:52	639	
grid19c.rsp	2020-04-03 10:51	1.7K	
hugespages_settings.sh	2020-04-03 10:56	1.2K	
limits.conf	2020-04-03 10:49	269	
ns01.ova	2020-04-03 10:32	710M	
oracle.sh	2020-04-03 10:50	149	
oragrid.sh	2020-04-03 10:50	150	
oraset	2020-04-03 10:55	1.6K	
rac01.ova	2020-04-03 10:33	636M	
rac02.ova	2020-04-03 10:34	632M	
sysctl.conf	2020-04-03 10:40	864	

Virtual Machines was created with VirtualBox. To import ova files use vboxmanage command. See below an example to load and install VM.

```
wget http://files.silverlake.space/ns01.ova
wget http://files.silverlake.space/rac01.ova
wget http://files.silverlake.space/rac02.ova
vboxmanage import ns01.ova
vboxmanage import rac01.ova
vboxmanage import rac02.ova
```

On VM just root account is configured. Password is *root01*. Access by ssh and IP.
- NS01 : 192.168.56.10
- RAC01 : 192.168.56.101
- RAC02 : 192.168.56.102

In this document for OS I use CentOS 7, free version of Red Hat 7. One of my customers use 15 000 stand-alone databases Oracle with CentOS without issue. During trainning and test, I also use CentOS. However in production, I advise to use Red Hat or Oracle Linux distributions.

Introduction

This procedure presents the installation of an Oracle RAC 19c cluster with 2 nodes. It is primarily intended for Oracle DBAs with a good culture on the functioning of a RAC cluster. System and network skills are essential. The objective here is to present a test model of an RAC cluster for training and in no way a production case. A production RAC cluster should not use VMs but physical servers and a suitable SAN and network infrastructure.

Version 19c introduced some changes compared to previous versions, notably on the installation of binaries and also on the network management between nodes.

In order to simulate a production case, no graphical interface will be used. All configuration is done from the command line via SSH (including VM management).

This platform was set up on a physical server having the following characteristics:

- CPU : Intel Xeon W3520 à 2.67GHz
- RAM : 32Go
- 2 disks de 2To

This server is configured in CentOS 7.7 with the installation of VirtualBox. The choice of VirtualBox is not compulsory, this product is simple and available for free on any OS. It is however useful to specify that the performances will remain very modest.

It is important to have enough RAM because each node of the cluster requires 8GB of RAM minimum.

The architecture is composed of 2 servers simulated by VMs (rac01 and rac02) with the following characteristics:

- 2 VCPUs
- RAM : 8Go
- 1 disk system of 50Go
- 1 disk of 50Go for Oracle's binaries (mount on /ora01)
- 5 network card

In addition a third VM, named NS01, is in place to ensure DNS management. A paragraph quickly presents the DNS configuration for this cluster. The DNS VM does not require a lot of resources:

- 1 VCPU
- RAM : 1Go
- 1 disk system of 8Go
- 1 network card

Here the virtualization used is VirtualBox. For VM RAC01 and RAC02 the first disk supports the Linux CentOS 7.7 OS and the second the Oracle Grid Infrastructure and RDBMS version 19.3 binaries.

Network cards enp0s3 et enp0S9 are aggregate -> bond0 and dedicated to public network

Network cards enp0s8 et enp0s10 dedicated to Interconnect (private) network → HAIP.

Network card enp0s16 dedicated to ASM network → flex cluster.

Shared disk space is configured as follows
- 6 disks of 20Go
- 6 disks of 50Go

The cluster is called alpha and is made up of the nodes rac01 and rac02. The diagram below shows the test cluster.

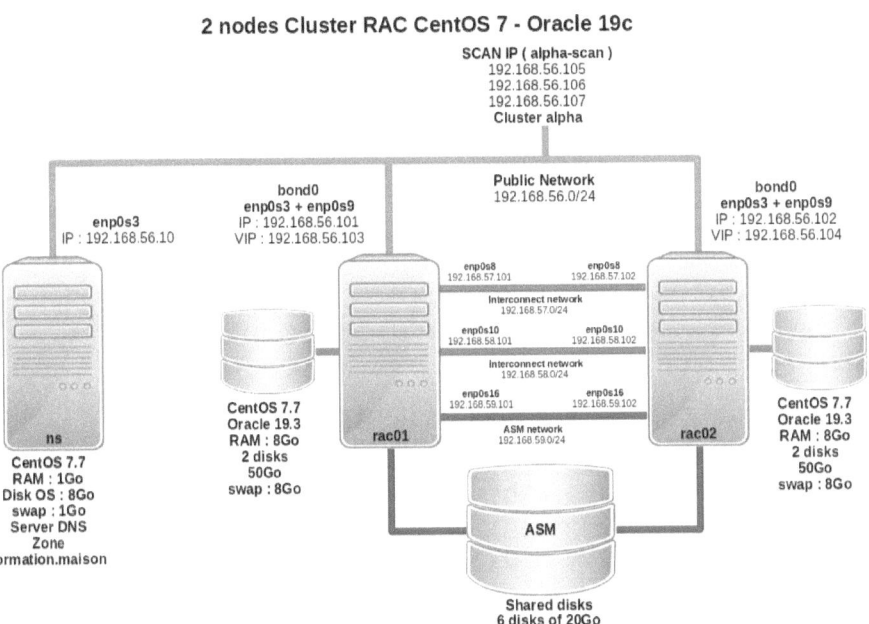

2 nodes Cluster RAC CentOS 7 - Oracle 19c

Name resolution is provided by a DNS server (IP: 192.168.56.10) in a fictitious area called formation.maison. The DNS configuration is briefly presented in the following paragraph. In a RAC cluster, DNS resolution is imperative.

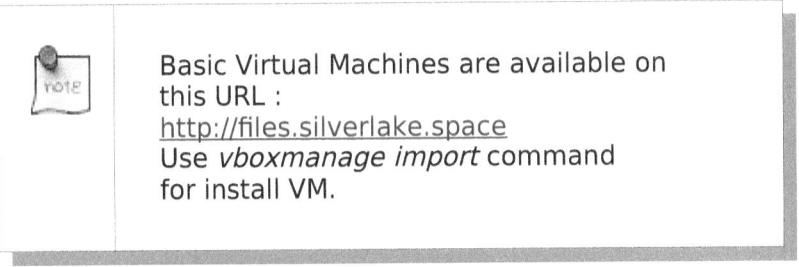

> Basic Virtual Machines are available on this URL :
> http://files.silverlake.space
> Use *vboxmanage import* command for install VM.

Repository RPM

In order to install the different packages on the VMs you need a repository. In this procedure the VMs do not have Internet access. The easiest way is to mount the distribution DVD on the VMs and configure yum to use the DVD as a repository. The following paragraph shows the method on VM NS01, for RAC01 and RAC02 the procedure is identical.

First, on the virtualization host, recover the ISO image of the CentOS 7 DVD. There are a large number of mirrors on the web allowing this. The following example uses a mirror on infoline.de.

```
wget
http://mirror.infonline.de/centos/7.7.1908/isos/x86_64/
CentOS-7-x86_64-DVD-1908.iso
```

Attach ISO at the VM

```
vboxmanage storageattach NS01 --storagectl IDE --port 0
--device 0 --type dvddrive --medium CentOS-7-x86_64-
DVD-1908.iso
```

Disable boot on DVD, just boot on hard disk.

```
vboxmanage modifyvm NS01 --boot1 disk
vboxmanage modifyvm NS01 --boot2 none
vboxmanage modifyvm NS01 --boot3 none
vboxmanage modifyvm NS01 --boot4 none
```

Lauch the VM and check for DVD.

```
lsblk
NAME     MAJ:MIN RM   SIZE RO TYPE MOUNTPOINT
sda        8:0    0     8G  0 disk
├─sda1     8:1    0     7G  0 part /
└─sda2     8:2    0     1G  0 part [SWAP]
sr0       11:0    1   4,4G  0 rom
sr1       11:1    1  1024M  0 rom
```

DVD is present on device /dev/sr0. Create a mount point and mount ISO

```
mkdir /centos
mount -o ro /dev/sr0 /centos
```

Check

```
df -h
Sys. de fichiers Taille Utilisé Dispo Uti% Monté sur
devtmpfs          486M       0  486M   0% /dev
tmpfs             496M       0  496M   0% /dev/shm
tmpfs             496M    6,7M  489M   2% /run
tmpfs             496M       0  496M   0%
/sys/fs/cgroup
/dev/sda1         6,8G    1,7G  4,7G  27% /
tmpfs             100M       0  100M   0% /run/user/0
/dev/sr0          4,4G    4,4G     0 100% /centos
```

Make this mount permanent.

```
cat /etc/mtab | grep centos >> /etc/fstab
```

Configure repository on this mount point. Go todirectory /etc/yum.repos.d and remove all files.

```
cd /etc/yum.repos.d
rm -f *
```

On this directory, create a file named dvd.repo with lines as follow:

```
[DVD]
name=DVD
baseurl=file:///centos
enabled=1
gpgcheck=0
```

Now yum use DVD to install packages DVD.

 Repeat the sames operations on VM RAC01 et RAC02

DNS

The configuration will be very simplified. VM NS01 just installed with the meta package core. The startup of this VM is as follows:

```
vboxmanage startvm NS01 --type headless
```

 Start on mode headless disable console.

Managing a DNS is a complex subject. This is to present the general principle and quickly have a DNS server. The domain will be formation.maison and the IP network 192.168.56.0/24. Install bind on VM NS01 (IP: 192.16.56.10).

```
yum -y install bind bind-utils
```

 Not start BIND before configuration.

There is a bind configuration file installed by default. Make it an archive.

```
mv /etc/named.conf /etc/named.conf.orig
```

Create a new file /etc/named.conf and put the following lines in it :

```
options {
    directory "/var/named";
};

zone "formation.maison" IN {
    type master;
    file "data/formation.maison.zone";
};

zone "56.168.192.in-addr.arpa" IN {
    type master;
    file "data/192.168.56.zone";
};
```

The directory clause of the options section indicates that you will have to look for the zone files under /var/named.

Configure zones

Under /var/named/data create file for resolution →
formation.maison.zone.

```
$ttl 38400
@  IN  SOA  ns.formation.maison.  root.formation.maison.
(
            2020032701 ;
            3600    ;
            3600 ;
            604800  ;
            86400 ) ;

@  IN  NS  ns.formation.maison.
ns             IN  A  192.168.56.10

rac01          IN  A  192.168.56.101
rac01-vip      IN  A  192.168.56.103
rac02          IN  A  192.168.56.102
rac02-vip      IN  A  192.168.56.104

alpha-scan     IN  A  192.168.56.105
alpha-scan     IN  A  192.168.56.106
alpha-scan     IN  A  192.168.56.107
```

Under /var/named/data create file reverse resolution →
192.168.56.zone

```
$ttl 38400
@  IN  SOA  ns.formation.maison.  root.formation.maison.
(
           2020032701 ;
           3600 ;
           3600 ;
           604800 ;
           86400 ) ;

@  IN  NS  ns.formation.maison.

10          IN  PTR  ns.formation.maison.

101         IN  PTR  rac01.formation.maison.
103         IN  PTR  rac01-vip.formation.maison.
102         IN  PTR  rac02.formation.maison.
104         IN  PTR  rac02-vip.formation.maison.

105         IN  PTR  alpha-scan.formation.maison.
106         IN  PTR  alpha-scan.formation.maison.
107         IN  PTR  alpha-scan.formation.maison.
```

Enable start of bind

```
systemctl start named
systemctl enable named
```

Prepare VM RAC01 and RAC02

The objective here is not to present the VirtualBox solution in detail. First, simply create 2 VMs, RAC01 and RAC2, very simply:

- 2 VCPU
- 8 Go of RAM
- 2 disks of 50Go
- 1 network card type host only on network 192.168.56.0/24

The other network cards as well as the shared disks will then be added by the vboxmanage command.

Install each VM by the DVD CentOS 7 → Minimal Install (meta package core).

The following actions relate to the management of networks and shared disks. They must be done VM stopped.

```
vboxmanage controlvm RAC01 poweroff
vboxmanage controlvm RAC02 poweroff
```

Networks configuration

As presented in the introduction, it is necessary to install a certain number of network cards on the cluster. In order to present a production type case, each VM will have 5 network cards.

The vboxmanage command creates these different interfaces. There is already a vboxnet0 interce created during the VM installation (IP: 192.168.56.1)

```
vboxmanage hostonlyif create
vboxmanage hostonlyif ipconfig vboxnet1 --ip
192.168.57.1
vboxmanage hostonlyif create
vboxmanage hostonlyif ipconfig vboxnet2 --ip
192.168.58.1
vboxmanage hostonlyif create
vboxmanage hostonlyif ipconfig vboxnet3 --ip
192.168.59.1
```

Check

```
vboxmanage list hostonlyifs
Name:            vboxnet0
GUID:            786f6276-656e-4074-8000-0a0027000000
```

```
DHCP:              Disabled
IPAddress:         192.168.56.1
NetworkMask:       255.255.255.0
IPV6Address:
IPV6NetworkMaskPrefixLength: 0
HardwareAddress: 0a:00:27:00:00:00
MediumType:        Ethernet
Wireless:          No
Status:            Up
VBoxNetworkName: HostInterfaceNetworking-vboxnet0

Name:              vboxnet1
GUID:              786f6276-656e-4174-8000-0a0027000001
DHCP:              Disabled
IPAddress:         192.168.57.1
NetworkMask:       255.255.255.0
IPV6Address:
IPV6NetworkMaskPrefixLength: 0
HardwareAddress: 0a:00:27:00:00:01
MediumType:        Ethernet
Wireless:          No
Status:            Up
VBoxNetworkName: HostInterfaceNetworking-vboxnet1

Name:              vboxnet2
GUID:              786f6276-656e-4274-8000-0a0027000002
DHCP:              Disabled
IPAddress:         192.168.58.1
NetworkMask:       255.255.255.0
IPV6Address:
IPV6NetworkMaskPrefixLength: 0
HardwareAddress: 0a:00:27:00:00:02
MediumType:        Ethernet
Wireless:          No
Status:            Up
VBoxNetworkName: HostInterfaceNetworking-vboxnet2

Name:              vboxnet3
GUID:              786f6276-656e-4374-8000-0a0027000003
DHCP:              Disabled
IPAddress:         192.168.59.1
NetworkMask:       255.255.255.0
IPV6Address:
IPV6NetworkMaskPrefixLength: 0
```

```
HardwareAddress: 0a:00:27:00:00:03
MediumType:      Ethernet
Wireless:        No
Status:          Up
VBoxNetworkName: HostInterfaceNetworking-vboxnet3
```

Then assign the interfaces to the VMs. The 3rd network card is properly assigned to the 192.168.56.0 network, vboxnet0 because a bond will be implemented (see below)

```
vboxmanage modifyvm RAC01 --hostonlyadapter2 vboxnet1
vboxmanage modifyvm RAC01 --nic2 hostonly
vboxmanage modifyvm RAC02 --hostonlyadapter2 vboxnet1
vboxmanage modifyvm RAC02 --nic2 hostonly

vboxmanage modifyvm RAC01 --hostonlyadapter3 vboxnet0
vboxmanage modifyvm RAC01 --nic3 hostonly
vboxmanage modifyvm RAC02 --hostonlyadapter3 vboxnet0
vboxmanage modifyvm RAC02 --nic3 hostonly

vboxmanage modifyvm RAC01 --hostonlyadapter4 vboxnet2
vboxmanage modifyvm RAC01 --nic4 hostonly
vboxmanage modifyvm RAC02 --hostonlyadapter4 vboxnet2
vboxmanage modifyvm RAC02 --nic4 hostonly

vboxmanage modifyvm RAC01 --hostonlyadapter5 vboxnet3
vboxmanage modifyvm RAC01 --nic5 hostonly
vboxmanage modifyvm RAC02 --hostonlyadapter5 vboxnet3
vboxmanage modifyvm RAC02 --nic5 hostonly
```

Shared disks

Here, the storage space managed by ASM will be set up in the form of a number of disks shared between the two nodes of the cluster. On Linux command vboxmanage can be write in lower case (vboxmanage or VBoxManage !).

Disks creation

```
for i in $(seq 1 6); do VBoxManage createemedium disk --
filename DISK0${i}.vdi --size 20000 --variant
Fixed;done
for i in $(seq 1 6); do VBoxManage modifymedium disk
DISK0${i}.vdi --type shareable;done
for i in $(seq 7 9); do VBoxManage createemedium disk --
filename DISK0${i}.vdi --size 50000 --variant
Fixed;done
for i in $(seq 7 9); do VBoxManage modifymedium disk
DISK0${i}.vdi --type shareable;done
for i in $(seq 10 12); do VBoxManage createemedium disk
--filename DISK${i}.vdi --size 50000 --variant
Fixed;done
for i in $(seq 10 12); do VBoxManage modifymedium disk
DISK${i}.vdi --type shareable;done
```

Attach disks to VM

```
for i in $(seq 1 9); do VBoxManage storageattach RAC01
--storagectl SATA --port ${i} --device 0 --type hdd --
medium DISK0${i}.vdi;done
for i in $(seq 10 12); do VBoxManage storageattach
RAC01 --storagectl SATA --port ${i} --device 0 --type
hdd --medium DISK${i}.vdi;done
for i in $(seq 1 9); do VBoxManage storageattach RAC02
--storagectl SATA --port ${i} --device 0 --type hdd --
medium DISK0${i}.vdi;done
for i in $(seq 10 12); do VBoxManage storageattach
RAC02 --storagectl SATA --port ${i} --device 0 --type
hdd --medium DISK${i}.vdi;done
```

Attach another disk

To finalize, create on each node a second disk with a size of 50Go. This disk will be use to install oracle's binaries.

On each VM port 1 is buzy by disk OS, ports 2 to 12 are buzy by shared disks. So you must use port 13.

For RAC01

```
vboxmanage createemedium disk --filename DISK2_RAC01.vdi
--size 50000 --variant Fixed
vboxmanage storageattach RAC01 --storagectl SATA --port
13 --device 0 --type hdd --medium DISK2_RAC01.vdi
```

For RAC02

```
vboxmanage createemedium disk --filename DISK2_RAC02.vdi
--size 50000 --variant Fixed
vboxmanage storageattach RAC02 --storagectl SATA --port
13 --device 0 --type hdd --medium DISK2_RAC02.vdi
```

Conclusion configuration VM

At this stage the VMs RAC01 and RAC02 are correctly configured, it is enough to start them.

```
vboxmanage startvm RAC01 --type headless
vboxmanage startvm RAC02 --type headless
```

The following actions will be performed with root connection on each machine.

System configuration

The servers are installed with the minimal Red Hat 7 OS (Metapackage Core). Only the root account is in place.

Users and Groups

Create 2 users

- oracle -> RDBMS
- oragrid -> Grid Infrastructure

Create groups

- oinstall : primary group for oragrid and oracle
- dba : connection as sysdba (user oracle)
- oper : connection as sysoper (user oracle)
- backupdba : user for backup (user oracle)
- dgdba : user for dataguard (user oracle)
- kmdba : user for encryption (user oracle)
- racdba : connexion as sysrac (user oracle)
- asmadmin : connection as sysasm (user oragrid)
- asmdba : connexction as sysdba (user oracle et oragrid)
- asmoper : connection as sysoper (user oragrid)

```
groupadd -g 1001 oinstall
groupadd -g 1002 dba
groupadd -g 1003 oper
groupadd -g 1004 backupdba
groupadd -g 1005 dgdba
groupadd -g 1006 kmdba
groupadd -g 1007 racdba
groupadd -g 1008 asmadmin
groupadd -g 1009 asmdba
groupadd -g 1010 asmoper
```

The numbering of the groups, gid, must be the same on all the nodes of the cluster.

The creation of the users also requires that the uid be identical on all the nodes.

User oracle

```
useradd -u 1001 -g oinstall -G
dba,oper,backupdba,dgdba,kmdba,racdba,asmdba -d
/home/oracle -s /bin/bash oracle
```

Affect password *oracle01* to user oracle

```
passwd oracle
```

User oragrid

```
useradd -u 1002 -g oinstall -G asmdba,asmadmin,asmoper
-d /home/oragrid -s /bin/bash oragrid
```

Affect password *oragrid01* to user oragrid

```
passwd oragrid
```

Storage

It is provided by two local hard disks on each server and a shared disk space including:

- 3 disks of 20Go : OCR et Voting Disk
- 3 disks of 20Go : Database MGMTDB
- 3 disks of 50Go : DATA
- 3 disks of 50Go : FRA (Fast Recovery Area)

The lsblk command allows you to view the disk configuration of each node.

```
lsblk
NAME     MAJ:MIN RM  SIZE RO TYPE MOUNTPOINT
sda       8:0     0   50G  0 disk
├─sda1    8:1     0    8G  0 part [SWAP]
└─sda2    8:2     0   42G  0 part /
sdb       8:16    0 19,5G  0 disk
sdc       8:32    0 19,5G  0 disk
sdd       8:48    0 19,5G  0 disk
sde       8:64    0 19,5G  0 disk
sdf       8:80    0 19,5G  0 disk
sdg       8:96    0 19,5G  0 disk
sdh       8:112   0 48,8G  0 disk
sdi       8:128   0 48,8G  0 disk
sdj       8:144   0 48,8G  0 disk
sdk       8:160   0 48,8G  0 disk
sdl       8:176   0 48,8G  0 disk
sdm       8:192   0 48,8G  0 disk
sdn       8:208   0   50G  0 disk
sr0      11:0     1 1024M  0 rom
```

Disk sda supporting OS.

Disks sdb to sdm dedicated to ASM

Disk sdn for Oracle's binairies

File-system

On each node create a primary partition on whole disk sdn.

```
parted -s -a optimal /dev/sdn mklabel msdos -- mkpart
primary  1 -1
```

Check

```
lsblk
NAME    MAJ:MIN RM   SIZE RO TYPE MOUNTPOINT
sda       8:0     0    50G  0 disk
├─sda1    8:1     0     8G  0 part [SWAP]
└─sda2    8:2     0    42G  0 part /
sdb       8:16    0  19,5G  0 disk
sdc       8:32    0  19,5G  0 disk
sdd       8:48    0  19,5G  0 disk
sde       8:64    0  19,5G  0 disk
sdf       8:80    0  19,5G  0 disk
sdg       8:96    0  19,5G  0 disk
sdh       8:112   0  48,8G  0 disk
sdi       8:128   0  48,8G  0 disk
sdj       8:144   0  48,8G  0 disk
sdk       8:160   0  48,8G  0 disk
sdl       8:176   0  48,8G  0 disk
sdm       8:192   0  48,8G  0 disk
sdn       8:208   0    50G  0 disk
└─sdn1    8:209   0    50G  0 part
sr0      11:0     1 1024M  0 rom
```

The partprobe command allows you
to re-read the partition table without the
need to reboot. To be used if the
information is not correct.

Make a file system on this partition and mount it on /ora01. Affect the good rights.

```
mkfs -t ext4 /dev/sdn1
mkdir /ora01
mount /dev/sdn1 /ora01
chown oragrid:oinstall /ora01
```

Add this in /etc/fstab

```
cat /etc/mtab | grep ora01 >> /etc/fstab
```

It is important to check in the event of fine partitioning that the mount points /usr and /var do not have the nosuid option positioned in the /etc/fstab file.

Still in /etc/fstab, you must configure the file-system /dev/shm correctly, the installer checks that this value is 2GB minimum.

```
...
tmpfs    /dev/shm  tmpfs    size=2G 0 0
...
```

Remount file-system

```
mount -o remount /dev/shm
```

Pre-configuration ASM

It is important to properly configure the disks for use with ASM. There are three possible methods:

- ASMLIB : requests the installation of specific Oracle packages. (obsolete in 19c)
- AFD : Available since version 12.1.0.2 which is the successor to ASMLIB.
- UDEV : UDEV rules have the advantage of independence from Oracle.

In this document the UDEV method will be implemented. Its general principle is to present the disk with the same device name to the OS and to assign the correct owner to it here, in this case oragrid groupe asmadmin.

First, on one of the nodes, locate the shared disks (here from sdb to sdm)

```
lsblk
NAME     MAJ:MIN RM   SIZE RO TYPE MOUNTPOINT
sda        8:0    0    50G  0 disk
├─sda1     8:1    0     8G  0 part [SWAP]
└─sda2     8:2    0    42G  0 part /
sdb        8:16   0  19,5G  0 disk
sdc        8:32   0  19,5G  0 disk
sdd        8:48   0  19,5G  0 disk
sde        8:64   0  19,5G  0 disk
sdf        8:80   0  19,5G  0 disk
sdg        8:96   0  19,5G  0 disk
sdh        8:112  0  48,8G  0 disk
sdi        8:128  0  48,8G  0 disk
sdj        8:144  0  48,8G  0 disk
sdk        8:160  0  48,8G  0 disk
sdl        8:176  0  48,8G  0 disk
sdm        8:192  0  48,8G  0 disk
sdn        8:208  0    50G  0 disk
└─sdn1     8:209  0    50G  0 part /ora01
sr0       11:0    1 1024M  0 rom
```

On these disks create a partition on the whole without formatting it.

This action is only to be done on one of the two nodes, for example rac01.

```
for i in b c d e f g h i j k l m; do parted -s -a
optimal /dev/sd${i} mklabel msdos -- mkpart primary  1
-1;done
```

Check

```
lsblk
NAME     MAJ:MIN RM   SIZE RO TYPE MOUNTPOINT
sda        8:0    0    50G  0 disk
├─sda1     8:1    0     8G  0 part [SWAP]
└─sda2     8:2    0    42G  0 part /
sdb        8:16   0  19,5G  0 disk
└─sdb1     8:17   0  19,5G  0 part
sdc        8:32   0  19,5G  0 disk
└─sdc1     8:33   0  19,5G  0 part
sdd        8:48   0  19,5G  0 disk
└─sdd1     8:49   0  19,5G  0 part
```

```
sde          8:64    0  19,5G   0  disk
└─sde1       8:65    0  19,5G   0  part
sdf          8:80    0  19,5G   0  disk
└─sdf1       8:81    0  19,5G   0  part
sdg          8:96    0  19,5G   0  disk
└─sdg1       8:97    0  19,5G   0  part
sdh          8:112   0  48,8G   0  disk
└─sdh1       8:113   0  48,8G   0  part
sdi          8:128   0  48,8G   0  disk
└─sdi1       8:129   0  48,8G   0  part
sdj          8:144   0  48,8G   0  disk
└─sdj1       8:145   0  48,8G   0  part
sdk          8:160   0  48,8G   0  disk
└─sdk1       8:161   0  48,8G   0  part
sdl          8:176   0  48,8G   0  disk
└─sdl1       8:177   0  48,8G   0  part
sdm          8:192   0  48,8G   0  disk
└─sdm1       8:193   0  48,8G   0  part
sdn          8:208   0    50G   0  disk
└─sdn1       8:209   0    50G   0  part /ora01
sr0         11:0     1  1024M   0  rom
```

On the other node use the partprobe command to re-read the disk partitions and check with the lsblk command.

On each node create the file /etc/udev/rules.d/99-oracleasm.rules. the following shell launched on each node generates this file

```
#!/bin/bash
rm -f /etc/udev/rules.d/99-oracleasm.rules
i=1
cmd="/usr/lib/udev/scsi_id -g -u -d"
for disk in sdb sdc sdd sde sdf sdg sdh sdi sdj sdk sdl
sdm; do
cat <<EOF >> /etc/udev/rules.d/99-oracleasm.rules
KERNEL=="sd?1", SUBSYSTEM=="block", PROGRAM=="$cmd
/dev/\$parent", RESULT=="`$cmd /dev/$disk`",
SYMLINK+="asm1$i", OWNER="oragrid", GROUP="asmadmin",
MODE="0660"
EOF
i=$(($i+1))
done
```

Check -> cat /etc/udev/rules.d/99-oracleasm.rules

```
KERNEL=="sd?1", SUBSYSTEM=="block", PROGRAM=="/usr/lib/
```

23

```
udev/scsi_id -g -u -d /dev/$parent",
RESULT=="1ATA_VBOX_HARDDISK_VB1dc9a0a8-16c90831",
SYMLINK+="asm01", OWNER="oragrid", GROUP="asmadmin",
MODE="0660"
KERNEL=="sd?1", SUBSYSTEM=="block", PROGRAM=="/usr/lib/
udev/scsi_id -g -u -d /dev/$parent",
RESULT=="1ATA_VBOX_HARDDISK_VB45289d49-f4e783e6",
SYMLINK+="asm02", OWNER="oragrid", GROUP="asmadmin",
MODE="0660"
KERNEL=="sd?1", SUBSYSTEM=="block", PROGRAM=="/usr/lib/
udev/scsi_id -g -u -d /dev/$parent",
RESULT=="1ATA_VBOX_HARDDISK_VB35f53803-76a94d1b",
SYMLINK+="asm03", OWNER="oragrid", GROUP="asmadmin",
MODE="0660"
KERNEL=="sd?1", SUBSYSTEM=="block", PROGRAM=="/usr/lib/
udev/scsi_id -g -u -d /dev/$parent",
RESULT=="1ATA_VBOX_HARDDISK_VB8e2c4429-343ad9c0",
SYMLINK+="asm04", OWNER="oragrid", GROUP="asmadmin",
MODE="0660"
KERNEL=="sd?1", SUBSYSTEM=="block", PROGRAM=="/usr/lib/
udev/scsi_id -g -u -d /dev/$parent",
RESULT=="1ATA_VBOX_HARDDISK_VB40904e0c-7e954467",
SYMLINK+="asm05", OWNER="oragrid", GROUP="asmadmin",
MODE="0660"
KERNEL=="sd?1", SUBSYSTEM=="block", PROGRAM=="/usr/lib/
udev/scsi_id -g -u -d /dev/$parent",
RESULT=="1ATA_VBOX_HARDDISK_VB744a4d20-22e96f33",
SYMLINK+="asm06", OWNER="oragrid", GROUP="asmadmin",
MODE="0660"
KERNEL=="sd?1", SUBSYSTEM=="block", PROGRAM=="/usr/lib/
udev/scsi_id -g -u -d /dev/$parent",
RESULT=="1ATA_VBOX_HARDDISK_VBca63a25e-4c414d08",
SYMLINK+="asm07", OWNER="oragrid", GROUP="asmadmin",
MODE="0660"
KERNEL=="sd?1", SUBSYSTEM=="block", PROGRAM=="/usr/lib/
udev/scsi_id -g -u -d /dev/$parent",
RESULT=="1ATA_VBOX_HARDDISK_VB44d7c37c-f9ed8df0",
SYMLINK+="asm08", OWNER="oragrid", GROUP="asmadmin",
MODE="0660"
KERNEL=="sd?1", SUBSYSTEM=="block", PROGRAM=="/usr/lib/
udev/scsi_id -g -u -d /dev/$parent",
RESULT=="1ATA_VBOX_HARDDISK_VB3c6a93ac-73d39443",
SYMLINK+="asm09", OWNER="oragrid", GROUP="asmadmin",
MODE="0660"
```

```
KERNEL=="sd?1", SUBSYSTEM=="block", PROGRAM=="/usr/lib/
udev/scsi_id -g -u -d /dev/$parent",
RESULT=="1ATA_VBOX_HARDDISK_VB5279d048-d41ed1f8",
SYMLINK+="asm10", OWNER="oragrid", GROUP="asmadmin",
MODE="0660"
KERNEL=="sd?1", SUBSYSTEM=="block", PROGRAM=="/usr/lib/
udev/scsi_id -g -u -d /dev/$parent",
RESULT=="1ATA_VBOX_HARDDISK_VBbed3e213-95ede212",
SYMLINK+="asm11", OWNER="oragrid", GROUP="asmadmin",
MODE="0660"
KERNEL=="sd?1", SUBSYSTEM=="block", PROGRAM=="/usr/lib/
udev/scsi_id -g -u -d /dev/$parent",
RESULT=="1ATA_VBOX_HARDDISK_VBcf127c1b-3ec57d4c",
SYMLINK+="asm12", OWNER="oragrid", GROUP="asmadmin",
MODE="0660"
```

Reload UDEV rules

```
udevadm control --reload-rules
udevadm trigger
```

Check

```
ll /dev/asm*
lrwxrwxrwx 1 root root 4 17 mars  17:48 /dev/asm01 ->
sdb1
lrwxrwxrwx 1 root root 4 17 mars  17:48 /dev/asm10 ->
sdk1
lrwxrwxrwx 1 root root 4 17 mars  17:48 /dev/asm11 ->
sdl1
lrwxrwxrwx 1 root root 4 17 mars  17:48 /dev/asm12 ->
sdm1
lrwxrwxrwx 1 root root 4 17 mars  17:48 /dev/asm02 ->
sdc1
lrwxrwxrwx 1 root root 4 17 mars  17:48 /dev/asm03 ->
sdd1
lrwxrwxrwx 1 root root 4 17 mars  17:48 /dev/asm04 ->
sde1
lrwxrwxrwx 1 root root 4 17 mars  17:48 /dev/asm05 ->
sdf1
lrwxrwxrwx 1 root root 4 17 mars  17:48 /dev/asm06 ->
sdg1
lrwxrwxrwx 1 root root 4 17 mars  17:48 /dev/asm07 ->
sdh1
lrwxrwxrwx 1 root root 4 17 mars  17:48 /dev/asm08 ->
sdi1
```

```
lrwxrwxrwx 1 root root 4 17 mars   17:48 /dev/asm09 ->
sdj1

ll /dev/sd?1
brw-rw---- 1 root      disk     8,   1 11 mars   07:20
/dev/sda1
brw-rw---- 1 oragrid asmadmin 8,  17 11 mars   07:20
/dev/sdb1
brw-rw---- 1 oragrid asmadmin 8,  33 11 mars   07:20
/dev/sdc1
brw-rw---- 1 oragrid asmadmin 8,  49 11 mars   07:20
/dev/sdd1
brw-rw---- 1 oragrid asmadmin 8,  65 11 mars   07:20
/dev/sde1
brw-rw---- 1 oragrid asmadmin 8,  81 11 mars   07:20
/dev/sdf1
brw-rw---- 1 oragrid asmadmin 8,  97 11 mars   07:20
/dev/sdg1
brw-rw---- 1 oragrid asmadmin 8, 113 11 mars   07:20
/dev/sdh1
brw-rw---- 1 oragrid asmadmin 8, 129 11 mars   07:20
/dev/sdi1
brw-rw---- 1 oragrid asmadmin 8, 145 11 mars   07:20
/dev/sdj1
brw-rw---- 1 oragrid asmadmin 8, 161 11 mars   07:20
/dev/sdk1
brw-rw---- 1 oragrid asmadmin 8, 177 11 mars   07:20
/dev/sdl1
brw-rw---- 1 oragrid asmadmin 8, 193 11 mars   07:20
/dev/sdm1
```

Packages

You must install different packages on each of the nodes.

```
yum install compat-libcap1 gcc gcc-c++ ksh libaio-devel
nfs-utils sysstat unzip bind-utils
yum -y install perl-TermReadKey xauth xdpyinfo
yum install vim-enhanced wget psmisc net-tools
```

Although in this example, the cluster management does not use any graphical interface, the X libraries are however required, otherwise a warning will be generated during the installation.

Oracle massively uses PERL scripts, especially if multitenant management is in place and we want to use pluggable databases. To pass certain SQL scripts, in particular catalog, catproc,... Oracle advises not to use SQL*Plus but catcon.pl. In the case of a minimal installation of Red Hat 7, an additional PERL module (**perl-TermReadKey**) must be installed, otherwise catcon fails.

Some packages are useful, see essential

- vim-enhanced powerfull editor.
- bind-utils content nslookup
- wget load a file from an URL.
- psmisc contint command pstree and fuser (mandatory for PSU)
- net-tools content command ifconfig

The documentation refer to the **compat-libstdc++-33** package, this is optional, a warning will be generated during installation. The compat-libstdc++-33 package (C ++ compatibility libraries) is not available in the standard Red Hat repositories, you must use the Optionnal repository or manually load the package. The following link allows you to load the rpm

```
wget
http://mirror.centos.org/centos/7/os/x86_64/Packages/co
mpat-libstdc++-33-3.2.3-72.el7.x86_64.rpm
```

Another useful package is rlwrap which allows you to use the direction arrows in Oracle tools (SQL * Plus, adrci, rman...). You must configure aliases: alias sqlplus='rlwrap sqlplus'... Like compat-libstdc++-33 it must be installed from an rpm found on the Net.

```
wget
https://download-ib01.fedoraproject.org/pub/epel/7/x86_
64/Packages/r/rlwrap-0.43-2.el7.x86_64.rpm
```

Kernel configuration

Oracle requires some tweaks to the Linux kernel, especially on memory management and semaphores. To make these parameters permanent, you must write them in the /etc/sysctl.conf file. Below the lines to add :

```
# Shared memory
kernel.shmall = 2097152
kernel.shmmax = 8589934592
kernel.shmmni = 4096

# Semaphores
kernel.sem = 250 32000 100 128

kernel.panic_on_oops = 1

# Files
fs.file-max = 6815744
fs.aio-max-nr = 1048576

# Network
net.ipv4.ip_local_port_range = 9000 65500
net.core.rmem_default = 262144
net.core.rmem_max = 4194304
net.core.wmem_default = 262144
net.core.wmem_max = 1048576

# Disable strict mode on Reverse Path Filtering for
HAIP
# Manadatory in RAC for kernel since 2.6.32. See MOS :
1286796.1
net.ipv4.conf.enp0s8.rp_filter = 2
net.ipv4.conf.enp0s10.rp_filter = 2
```

```
# Disable IPV6
net.ipv6.conf.all.disable_ipv6 = 1
net.ipv6.conf.default.disable_ipv6 = 1

# Memory optimisation
vm.swappiness = 1
vm.dirty_background_ratio = 3
vm.dirty_ratio = 80
vm.dirty_expire_centisecs = 500
vm.dirty_writeback_centisecs = 100
```

- The values type shm relate to the Shared Memory, therefore the SGA of Oracle.
- The sem type values relate to the semaphores therefore linked to the PROCESSES parameter of Oracle.
- Net type values are relative to the network. The net.ipv4.conf.enp0s8 (enp0s10) .rp_filter = 2 clause is mandatory on a RAC using multiple interfaces for the Interconnect network from 2.6.32 linux kernels. For more info see MOS note: 1286796.1
- The values type vm relate to the memory and in particular to the management of dirty blocks in the database buffer cache.

Activate configuration by this command :

```
sysctl -p
```

Limits

The limits relate to the resources used by a particular user, in this case oracle. The number of open processes and files is affected. Add the following lines to the /etc/security/limits.conf file

```
@oinstall soft nproc 16384
@oinstall hard nproc 16384
@oinstall soft nofile 1024
@oinstall hard nofile 65536
@oinstall soft stack 10240
@oinstall hard stack 32768
oracle soft memlock 134217728
oracle hard memlock 134217728
```

These limits do not affect performance. However, they can hinder their proper functioning.

The soft limit of a user can be modified by the user himself, but without however exceeding the hard limit. This configuration allows defining the soft and hard limits of a user. The ulimit command allows a user to change their limits for the current shell.

> On the memlock clause do not use the oinstall group as for the other values, but use the user oracle otherwise there will be a failure (not blocking) at installation.

Modify file /etc/pam.d/login and add this line : :

```
session required pam_limits.so
```

In directory /etc/profile.d create file oracle.sh with lines belows :

```
if [ $USER = "oracle" ]; then
  if [ $SHELL = "/bin/ksh" ]; then
    ulimit -p 16384
    ulimit -n 65536
  else
    ulimit -u 16384 -n 65536
  fi
fi
```

Always in /etc/profile.d create file oragrid.sh with lines belows :

```
if [ $USER = "oragrid" ]; then
  if [ $SHELL = "/bin/ksh" ]; then
    ulimit -p 16384
    ulimit -n 65536
  else
    ulimit -u 16384 -n 65536
  fi
fi
```

SELinux

Oracle has been compatible with SELinux since 12c, so it is advisable to leave the default value, ie Enforcing, in place.

It is still possible to completely deactivate SELinux by editing the /etc/selinux/config file and by setting the SELINUX clause to disabled.

Firewall

Firewall management in RedHat 7 uses firewalld which implements the iptables rules. For the sake of simplification, deactivate the firewall.

```
systemctl stop firewalld
systemctl disable firewalld
```

Network

Network management in a RAC cluster requires special care. Many installation and performance concerns are due to a bad configuration mainly on the Interconnect network.

First add the following line to the file /etc/sysconfig/network

```
NOZEROCONF=yes
```

The NOZEROCONF = yes clause is not mandatory on a stand-alone server, but imperative on a RAC cluster. Since version 11.2.0.2, cluster management uses addresses of the APIPA type (169.254.0.0/16) for the interconnect interface, so it is vital that the OS cannot manage this type of address. This also explains why the avahi daemon must be disabled in a RAC. The following diagram shows the network cabling carried out.

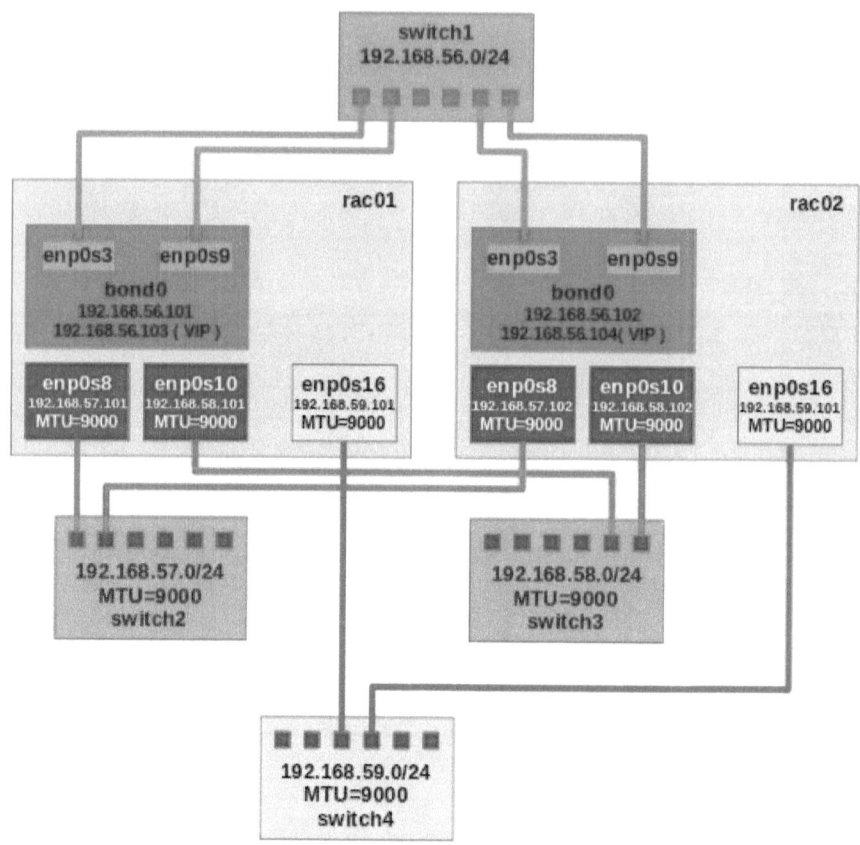

The servers have 5 network cards. The cards enp0s3 and enp0s9 are grouped together in a bond, below the configuration of the bond.

File ifcfg-bond0

```
DEVICE=bond0
BONDING_MASTER=yes
BOOTPROTO=none
ONBOOT=yes
BROADCAST=192.168.56.255
NETWORK=192.168.56.0
BONDING_OPTS="miimon=100 mode=active-backup
fail_over_mac=1"
IPADDR=192.168.56.101
PREFIX=24
GATEWAY=192.168.56.1
DNS1=192.168.56.10
```

```
DOMAIN=formation.maison
```

Clause fail_over_mac=1 is mandatory on VM VirtualBox.

File ifcfg-enp0s3

```
DEVICE=enp0s3
ONBOOT=yes
BOOTPROTO=none
MASTER=bond0
SLAVE=yes
```

File ifcfg-enp0s9

```
DEVICE=enp0s9
ONBOOT=yes
BOOTPROTO=none
MASTER=bond0
SLAVE=yes
```

The network cards enp0s8 and enp0s10 are dedicated to interconnect. By default, Ethernet frames have an MTU of 1500 bytes. It is recommended by Oracle and for the Interconnect network to modify this value. The Oracle blocks making a size of 8Ko a fragmentation is therefore necessary (6 frames of 1500 bytes) which is CPU consuming. By activating the Jumbo Frames at a value of 9Ko there is no more fragmentation. Below the configuration of the two interconnect cards.

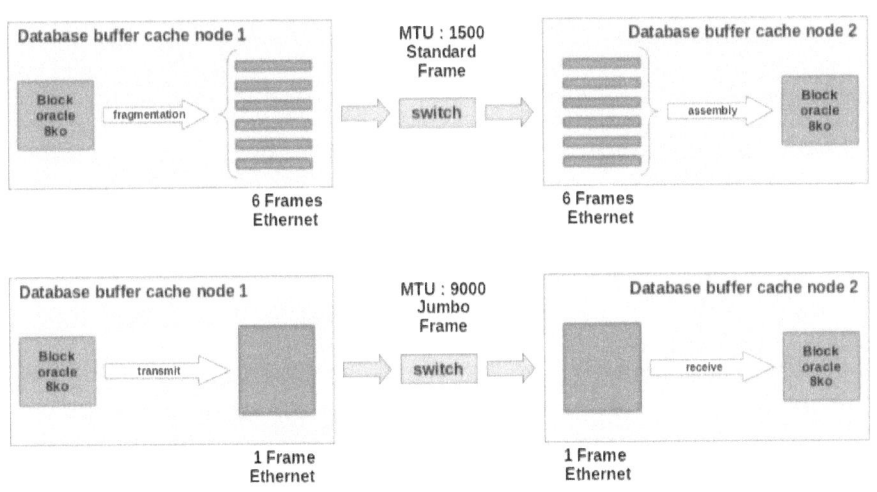

File ifcfg-enpOs8

```
IPADDR=192.168.57.101
NETMASK=255.255.255.0
BOOTPROTO=static
DEVICE=enpOs8
ONBOOT=yes
MTU=9000
```

File ifcfg-enpOs10

```
IPADDR=192.168.58.101
NETMASK=255.255.255.0
BOOTPROTO=static
DEVICE=enpOs10
ONBOOT=yes
MTU=9000
```

There remains the configuration of the 5th network card, enpOs16. Version 19c introduces the systematic use of a network dedicated to ASM management (flex cluster concept). Although it is possible to use the Interconnect network to do this, it is advisable to use a dedicated ASM network.

File ifcfg-enpOs16

```
IPADDR=192.168.59.101
NETMASK=255.255.255.0
BOOTPROTO=static
DEVICE=enpOs16
ONBOOT=yes
MTU=9000
```

As with the Interconnect network, jumbo frames are activated on the ASM network.

Check on RAC01

```
[root@rac01 ~]# ip a
1: lo: <LOOPBACK,UP,LOWER_UP> mtu 65536 qdisc noqueue
state UNKNOWN group default qlen 1000
    link/loopback 00:00:00:00:00:00 brd
00:00:00:00:00:00
    inet 127.0.0.1/8 scope host lo
       valid_lft forever preferred_lft forever
2: enpOs3: <BROADCAST,MULTICAST,SLAVE,UP,LOWER_UP> mtu
1500 qdisc pfifo_fast master bond0 state UP group
default qlen 1000
```

```
      link/ether 08:00:27:1c:71:68 brd ff:ff:ff:ff:ff:ff
3: enp0s8: <BROADCAST,MULTICAST,UP,LOWER_UP> mtu 9000
qdisc pfifo_fast state UP group default qlen 1000
      link/ether 08:00:27:46:d8:76 brd ff:ff:ff:ff:ff:ff
    inet 192.168.57.101/24 brd 192.168.57.255 scope
global noprefixroute enp0s8
       valid_lft forever preferred_lft forever
4: enp0s9: <BROADCAST,MULTICAST,SLAVE,UP,LOWER_UP> mtu
1500 qdisc pfifo_fast master bond0 state UP group
default qlen 1000
    link/ether 08:00:27:74:d9:01 brd ff:ff:ff:ff:ff:ff
5: enp0s10: <BROADCAST,MULTICAST,UP,LOWER_UP> mtu 9000
qdisc pfifo_fast state UP group default qlen 1000
      link/ether 08:00:27:f0:ec:9f brd ff:ff:ff:ff:ff:ff
    inet 192.168.58.101/24 brd 192.168.58.255 scope
global noprefixroute enp0s10
       valid_lft forever preferred_lft forever
6: enp0s16: <BROADCAST,MULTICAST,UP,LOWER_UP> mtu 9000
qdisc pfifo_fast state UP group default qlen 1000
      link/ether 08:00:27:14:40:1c brd ff:ff:ff:ff:ff:ff
    inet 192.168.59.101/24 brd 192.168.59.255 scope
global noprefixroute enp0s16
       valid_lft forever preferred_lft forever
8: bond0: <BROADCAST,MULTICAST,MASTER,UP,LOWER_UP> mtu
1500 qdisc noqueue state UP group default qlen 1000
    link/ether 08:00:27:1c:71:68 brd ff:ff:ff:ff:ff:ff
    inet 192.168.56.101/24 brd 192.168.56.255 scope
global noprefixroute bond0
       valid_lft forever preferred_lft forever
[root@rac01 ~]#
```

On RAC02 configurations are identical, just IP changed.

```
[root@rac02 ~]# ip a
1: lo: <LOOPBACK,UP,LOWER_UP> mtu 65536 qdisc noqueue
state UNKNOWN group default qlen 1000
    link/loopback 00:00:00:00:00:00 brd
00:00:00:00:00:00
    inet 127.0.0.1/8 scope host lo
       valid_lft forever preferred_lft forever
2: enp0s3: <BROADCAST,MULTICAST,SLAVE,UP,LOWER_UP> mtu
1500 qdisc pfifo_fast master bond0 state UP group
default qlen 1000
    link/ether 08:00:27:ca:c3:ff brd ff:ff:ff:ff:ff:ff
3: enp0s8: <BROADCAST,MULTICAST,UP,LOWER_UP> mtu 9000
```

```
qdisc pfifo_fast state UP group default qlen 1000
    link/ether 08:00:27:67:f7:e9 brd ff:ff:ff:ff:ff:ff
    inet 192.168.57.102/24 brd 192.168.57.255 scope
global noprefixroute enp0s8
       valid_lft forever preferred_lft forever
4: enp0s9: <BROADCAST,MULTICAST,SLAVE,UP,LOWER_UP> mtu
1500 qdisc pfifo_fast master bond0 state UP group
default qlen 1000
    link/ether 08:00:27:f7:79:e1 brd ff:ff:ff:ff:ff:ff
5: enp0s10: <BROADCAST,MULTICAST,UP,LOWER_UP> mtu 9000
qdisc pfifo_fast state UP group default qlen 1000
    link/ether 08:00:27:c8:d7:82 brd ff:ff:ff:ff:ff:ff
    inet 192.168.58.102/24 brd 192.168.58.255 scope
global noprefixroute enp0s10
       valid_lft forever preferred_lft forever
6: enp0s16: <BROADCAST,MULTICAST,UP,LOWER_UP> mtu 9000
qdisc pfifo_fast state UP group default qlen 1000
    link/ether 08:00:27:28:55:16 brd ff:ff:ff:ff:ff:ff
    inet 192.168.59.102/24 brd 192.168.59.255 scope
global noprefixroute enp0s16
       valid_lft forever preferred_lft forever
8: bond0: <BROADCAST,MULTICAST,MASTER,UP,LOWER_UP> mtu
1500 qdisc noqueue state UP group default qlen 1000
    link/ether 08:00:27:ca:c3:ff brd ff:ff:ff:ff:ff:ff
    inet 192.168.56.102/24 brd 192.168.56.255 scope
global noprefixroute bond0
       valid_lft forever preferred_lft forever
[root@rac02 ~]#
```

Name resolution is vital, the /etc/resolv.conf file must correctly present the DNS and the default domains.

```
nameserver 192.168.56.10
search formation.maison
```

Below is the result of the nslookup command on the different cluster names

```
[root@rac02 ~]# nslookup alpha-scan
Server:         192.168.56.10
Address:     192.168.56.10#53

Name: alpha-scan.formation.maison
Address: 192.168.56.107
Name: alpha-scan.formation.maison
Address: 192.168.56.106
```

```
Name: alpha-scan.formation.maison
Address: 192.168.56.105

[root@rac02 ~]# nslookup rac01
Server:         192.168.56.10
Address:    192.168.56.10#53

Name: rac01.formation.maison
Address: 192.168.56.101

[root@rac02 ~]# nslookup rac02
Server:         192.168.56.10
Address:    192.168.56.10#53

Name: rac02.formation.maison
Address: 192.168.56.102

[root@rac02 ~]# nslookup rac01-vip
Server:         192.168.56.10
Address:    192.168.56.10#53

Name: rac01-vip.formation.maison
Address: 192.168.56.103

[root@rac02 ~]# nslookup rac02-vip
Server:         192.168.56.10
Address:    192.168.56.10#53

Name: rac02-vip.formation.maison
Address: 192.168.56.104

[root@rac02 ~]#
```

Time server NTP

The configuration of time synchronization is vital on a RAC without that the installation fails. Red Hat / CentOS version 7 uses chrony for time synchronization. Here the principle is to define the DNS server (ns.formation.maison) as a reference and to synchronize rac01 and rac02 on it.

You must install the chrony package on all three servers.

```
yum -y install chrony
```

On server ns.formation.maison (192.168.56.10) create file /etc/chrony.conf

```
local stratum 8
manual
allow 192.168.56.0/24
```

Start chrony

```
systemctl start chronyd
systemctl enable chronyd
```

On servers rac01 and rac02 create file /etc/chrony.conf

```
server ns
logdir /var/log/chrony
log measurements statistics tracking
```

Start chrony

```
systemctl start chronyd
systemctl enable chronyd
```

Command chronyc tracking to check

```
chronyc tracking
Reference ID    : C0A8380A (ns.formation.maison)
Stratum         : 9
Ref time (UTC)  : Wed Mar 18 08:08:05 2020
System time     : 0.000000006 seconds fast of NTP time
Last offset     : -0.000051367 seconds
RMS offset      : 0.000026241 seconds
Frequency       : 0.001 ppm fast
Residual freq   : -0.013 ppm
Skew            : 0.013 ppm
Root delay      : 0.000602176 seconds
Root dispersion : 0.000808289 seconds
Update interval : 1024.4 seconds
Leap status     : Normal
```

Binaries installation

We must install two product : :

- Grid Infrastructure
- RDBMS

Version 19c has slightly changed the usual installation mode. The files are pre-compiled, you have to unzip a zip in the future directory and launch the runInstaller.

Binaries are retrieved from the Oracle site.
https://www.oracle.com/database/technologies/oracle19c-linux-downloads.html

Oracle Database 19c (19.3) for Linux x86-64

Download	Description
LINUX X64_193000_db_home.zip	(3,059,705,302 bytes) (sha256sum - ba8329c757133da313ed3b6d7f86c5ac42cd9970a28bf2e6253f3235233aa8d8)

Directions
Installation guides and general Oracle Database 19c documentation are here.

Oracle Database 19c Grid Infrastructure (19.3) for Linux x86-64

Download	Description
LINUX_X64_193000_grid_home.zip	(2,889,184,573 bytes) (sha256sum - d668002664d9399cf61eb03c0d1e3687121fc890b1ddd50b35dcbe13c5307d2e)

Contains the Grid Infrastructure Software including Oracle Clusterware, Automated Storage Management (ASM), and ASM Cluster File System. Download and install prior to installing Oracle Real Application Clusters, Oracle Real Application Clusters One Node, or other application software in a Grid Environment.

The two zip files are on the rac01 server in the /INSTALL directory. There is no need to copy them to rac02 this will be done by the runInstaller.

Installation of Grid Infrastructure

As root on each node create the file /etc/oraInst.loc with the following lines:

```
inventory_loc=/ora01/app/oraInventory
inst_group=oinstall
```

Without this file there will be an error (not blocking) during installation.

```
ERROR:
PRVG-10467 : The default Oracle Inventory group could
not be determined.
```

This error is of no consequence, however, because the file is created automatically.

Change rights

```
chown oracle:oinstall /etc/oraInst.loc
chmod 0664 /etc/oraInst.loc
```

Connect oragrid on each node and create the following directories:

```
mkdir -p /ora01/app/oracle
mkdir -p /ora01/app/oragrid/product/19/GI
```

Connect to the rac01 server in oragrid and decompress the zip file of the Grid Infrastructure.

```
cd /ora01/app/oragrid/product/19/GI
unzip /INSTALL/LINUX.X64_193000_grid_home.zip
```

Install on rac01 lthis file (connection root)

```
cd /ora01/app/oragrid/product/19/GI/cv/rpm
yum -y install cvuqdisk-1.0.10-1.rpm
```

For rac02 simply copy this rpm from rac01 and install it via yum

SSH Keys

It is necessary to generate the SSH keys for the user oragrid and this on each node. Then it is necessary to transfer these keys between the nodes so that the connection is transparent. Oracle offers a utility to do this. From the rac01 node in the following directory:

```
cd /ora01/app/oragrid/product/19/GI/oui/prov/resources/
scripts
./sshUserSetup.sh -user oragrid -hosts "rac01 rac02" -
advanced -confirm -noPromptPassphrase
```

4 times the utility will ask for the password oragrid (here oragrid01). It is advisable to launch the runcluvfy utility to validate that everything is correct in terms of prerequisites.

```
cd /ora01/app/oragrid/product/19/GI
./runcluvfy.sh stage -pre crsinst -fixupnoexec -n
rac01,rac02 -verbose -method root | tee
$HOME/cluvfy.pre.log
```

40

You will then be asked for the root password (here *root01*) in order to verify the RPM Package Manager database.

On the rac01 server as oragrid and under $HOME create the response file -> grid19c.rsp

```
oracle.install.responseFileVersion=/oracle/install/
rspfmt_crsinstall_response_schema_v19.0.0
INVENTORY_LOCATION=/ora01/app/oraInventory
oracle.install.option=CRS_CONFIG
ORACLE_BASE=/ora01/app/oracle
oracle.install.asm.OSDBA=asmdba
oracle.install.asm.OSOPER=asmoper
oracle.install.asm.OSASM=asmadmin
oracle.install.crs.config.scanType=LOCAL_SCAN
oracle.install.crs.config.gpnp.scanName=alpha-scan
oracle.install.crs.config.gpnp.scanPort=1521
oracle.install.crs.config.ClusterConfiguration=STANDALO
NE
oracle.install.crs.config.configureAsExtendedCluster=fa
lse
oracle.install.crs.config.clusterName=alpha
oracle.install.crs.config.gpnp.configureGNS=false
oracle.install.crs.config.autoConfigureClusterNodeVIP=f
alse
oracle.install.crs.config.clusterNodes=rac01:rac01-
vip,rac02:rac02-vip
oracle.install.crs.config.networkInterfaceList=bond0:19
2.168.56.0:1,enp0s8:192.168.57.0:2,enp0s10:192.168.58.0
:2,enp0s16:192.168.56.59.0:4
oracle.install.crs.configureGIMR=true
oracle.install.asm.configureGIMRDataDG=true
oracle.install.crs.config.useIPMI=false
oracle.install.asm.SYSASMPassword=Manager19#
oracle.install.asm.diskGroup.name=OCR_VOTING
oracle.install.asm.diskGroup.redundancy=NORMAL
oracle.install.asm.diskGroup.AUSize=4
oracle.install.asm.diskGroup.disks=/dev/asm01,/dev/asm0
2,/dev/asm03
oracle.install.asm.diskGroup.diskDiscoveryString=/dev/a
sm*
oracle.install.asm.monitorPassword=Manager19#
oracle.install.asm.gimrDG.name=MGMTDB
oracle.install.asm.gimrDG.redundancy=NORMAL
oracle.install.asm.gimrDG.AUSize=4
```

```
oracle.install.asm.gimrDG.disks=/dev/asm04,/dev/asm05,/
dev/asm06
oracle.install.asm.configureAFD=false
oracle.install.crs.configureRHPS=false
oracle.install.crs.rootconfig.executeRootScript=false
```

It is also interesting to launch the runInstaller to validate the prerequisites from the response file

```
./gridSetup.sh -silent -responseFile
/home/oragrid/grid19c.rsp -executePrereqs
```

Here we find the previous warning

```
INFO:  [Feb 28, 2020 9:23:01 AM] *************** End of
CVU Error logs ***************
INFO:  [Feb 28, 2020 9:23:01 AM] All forked task are
completed at state init
INFO:  [Feb 28, 2020 9:23:01 AM] -----------------List
of failed Tasks-----------------
INFO:  [Feb 28, 2020 9:23:01 AM]
***************************************************
INFO:  [Feb 28, 2020 9:23:01 AM] RPM Package Manager
database: Verifies the RPM Package Manager database
files
INFO:  [Feb 28, 2020 9:23:01 AM] Severity:INFORMATION
INFO:  [Feb 28, 2020 9:23:01 AM]
OverallStatus:INFORMATION
INFO:  [Feb 28, 2020 9:23:01 AM] ----------------End
of failed Tasks List---------------
```

This action creates the logs directory in /ora01/app/oraInventory. It is advisable to remove it before installation

```
rm -rf /ora01/app/oraInventory/logs
```

If everything is correct launch the runInstaller

```
./gridSetup.sh -silent -responseFile
/home/oragrid/grid19c.rsp -waitforcompletion
```

 Disregard the warning on optional prerequisites, it does not interfere with the installation of the Grid Infrastructure.

As root on each node pass the following script, on rac01 first and then rac02

```
/ora01/app/oragrid/product/19/GI/root.sh
```

The root.sh script is a bit long …

On rac01 while monitoring the log file indicated at a time these lines should appear.

```
...
2020/03/18 11:09:46 CLSRSC-594: Executing installation
step 16 of 19: 'InitConfig'.

ASM a été créé et démarré.

[DBT-30001] Groupes de disques créés. Pour plus de
détails, consultez /ora01/app/oracle/cfgtoollogs/asmca/
asmca-200318AM111024.log.

2020/03/18 11:11:35 CLSRSC-482: Running command:
'/ora01/app/oragrid/product/19/GI/bin/ocrconfig -
upgrade oragrid oinstall'
CRS-4256: Updating the profile
Successful addition of voting disk
6c9e8aa632674fafbf22c84deb226068.
Successful addition of voting disk
5a31cc075a5e4f58bf90ba06cc1cdf29.
Successful addition of voting disk
edc04fcf879b4f25bf6efab8f15558c0.
Successfully replaced voting disk group with
+OCR_VOTING.
CRS-4256: Updating the profile
CRS-4266: Voting file(s) successfully replaced
##  STATE    File Universal Id                  File Name
Disk group
--  -----    -----------------                  --------
---------
 1. ONLINE   6c9e8aa632674fafbf22c84deb226068
(/dev/asm03) [OCR_VOTING]
 2. ONLINE   5a31cc075a5e4f58bf90ba06cc1cdf29
(/dev/asm02) [OCR_VOTING]
 3. ONLINE   edc04fcf879b4f25bf6efab8f15558c0
(/dev/asm01) [OCR_VOTING]
Located 3 voting disk(s).
...
```

Once these scripts have passed as root, go back to rac01 in oragrid and run the following script

```
/ora01/app/oragrid/product/19/GI/gridSetup.sh -
executeConfigTools -responseFile
/home/oragrid/grid19c.rsp -silent
```

This script notably creates the MGMTDB database (as PDB) and at the end performs a cluvfy in order to test the whole cluster. This script is also quite long.

When finished, add the following line in /etc/oratab on rac01

```
+ASM1:/ora01/app/oragrid/product/19/GI:N
```

Add the following line in /etc/oratab on rac02

```
+ASM2:/ora01/app/oragrid/product/19/GI:N
```

Test cluster resources

```
[oragrid@rac01 ~]$ . oraenv
ORACLE_SID = [oragrid] ? +ASM1
The Oracle base has been set to /ora01/app/oracle
[oragrid@rac01 ~]$ crsctl stat res -t
```

With connection on each node, it is possible to see IP configuration.

On RAC01

```
[root@rac01 ~]# ip a
1: lo: <LOOPBACK,UP,LOWER_UP> mtu 65536 qdisc noqueue
state UNKNOWN group default qlen 1000
    link/loopback 00:00:00:00:00:00 brd
00:00:00:00:00:00
    inet 127.0.0.1/8 scope host lo
       valid_lft forever preferred_lft forever
2: enp0s3: <BROADCAST,MULTICAST,SLAVE,UP,LOWER_UP> mtu
1500 qdisc pfifo_fast master bond0 state UP group
default qlen 1000
    link/ether 08:00:27:1c:71:68 brd ff:ff:ff:ff:ff:ff
3: enp0s8: <BROADCAST,MULTICAST,UP,LOWER_UP> mtu 9000
qdisc pfifo_fast state UP group default qlen 1000
    link/ether 08:00:27:46:d8:76 brd ff:ff:ff:ff:ff:ff
    inet 192.168.57.101/24 brd 192.168.57.255 scope
global noprefixroute enp0s8
       valid_lft forever preferred_lft forever
    inet 169.254.0.68/20 brd 169.254.15.255 scope
```

```
global enp0s8:1
        valid_lft forever preferred_lft forever
4: enp0s9: <BROADCAST,MULTICAST,SLAVE,UP,LOWER_UP> mtu
1500 qdisc pfifo_fast master bond0 state UP group
default qlen 1000
    link/ether 08:00:27:74:d9:01 brd ff:ff:ff:ff:ff:ff
5: enp0s10: <BROADCAST,MULTICAST,UP,LOWER_UP> mtu 9000
qdisc pfifo_fast state UP group default qlen 1000
    link/ether 08:00:27:f0:ec:9f brd ff:ff:ff:ff:ff:ff
    inet 192.168.58.101/24 brd 192.168.58.255 scope
global noprefixroute enp0s10
        valid_lft forever preferred_lft forever
    inet 169.254.31.226/20 brd 169.254.31.255 scope
global enp0s10:1
        valid_lft forever preferred_lft forever
6: enp0s16: <BROADCAST,MULTICAST,UP,LOWER_UP> mtu 9000
qdisc pfifo_fast state UP group default qlen 1000
    link/ether 08:00:27:14:40:1c brd ff:ff:ff:ff:ff:ff
    inet 192.168.59.101/24 brd 192.168.59.255 scope
global noprefixroute enp0s16
        valid_lft forever preferred_lft forever
7: bond0: <BROADCAST,MULTICAST,MASTER,UP,LOWER_UP> mtu
1500 qdisc noqueue state UP group default qlen 1000
    link/ether 08:00:27:74:d9:01 brd ff:ff:ff:ff:ff:ff
    inet 192.168.56.101/24 brd 192.168.56.255 scope
global noprefixroute bond0
        valid_lft forever preferred_lft forever
    inet 192.168.56.107/24 brd 192.168.56.255 scope
global secondary bond0:1
        valid_lft forever preferred_lft forever
    inet 192.168.56.106/24 brd 192.168.56.255 scope
global secondary bond0:3
        valid_lft forever preferred_lft forever
    inet 192.168.56.103/24 brd 192.168.56.255 scope
global secondary bond0:5
        valid_lft forever preferred_lft forever
```

On RAC02

```
[root@rac02 ~]# ip a
1: lo: <LOOPBACK,UP,LOWER_UP> mtu 65536 qdisc noqueue
state UNKNOWN group default qlen 1000
    link/loopback 00:00:00:00:00:00 brd
00:00:00:00:00:00
    inet 127.0.0.1/8 scope host lo
```

```
        valid_lft forever preferred_lft forever
2: enp0s3: <BROADCAST,MULTICAST,SLAVE,UP,LOWER_UP> mtu
1500 qdisc pfifo_fast master bond0 state UP group
default qlen 1000
    link/ether 08:00:27:ca:c3:ff brd ff:ff:ff:ff:ff:ff
3: enp0s8: <BROADCAST,MULTICAST,UP,LOWER_UP> mtu 9000
qdisc pfifo_fast state UP group default qlen 1000
    link/ether 08:00:27:67:f7:e9 brd ff:ff:ff:ff:ff:ff
    inet 192.168.57.102/24 brd 192.168.57.255 scope
global noprefixroute enp0s8
        valid_lft forever preferred_lft forever
    inet 169.254.10.21/20 brd 169.254.15.255 scope
global enp0s8:1
        valid_lft forever preferred_lft forever
4: enp0s9: <BROADCAST,MULTICAST,SLAVE,UP,LOWER_UP> mtu
1500 qdisc pfifo_fast master bond0 state UP group
default qlen 1000
    link/ether 08:00:27:f7:79:e1 brd ff:ff:ff:ff:ff:ff
5: enp0s10: <BROADCAST,MULTICAST,UP,LOWER_UP> mtu 9000
qdisc pfifo_fast state UP group default qlen 1000
    link/ether 08:00:27:c8:d7:82 brd ff:ff:ff:ff:ff:ff
    inet 192.168.58.102/24 brd 192.168.58.255 scope
global noprefixroute enp0s10
        valid_lft forever preferred_lft forever
    inet 169.254.16.178/20 brd 169.254.31.255 scope
global enp0s10:1
        valid_lft forever preferred_lft forever
6: enp0s16: <BROADCAST,MULTICAST,UP,LOWER_UP> mtu 9000
qdisc pfifo_fast state UP group default qlen 1000
    link/ether 08:00:27:28:55:16 brd ff:ff:ff:ff:ff:ff
    inet 192.168.59.102/24 brd 192.168.59.255 scope
global noprefixroute enp0s16
        valid_lft forever preferred_lft forever
7: bond0: <BROADCAST,MULTICAST,MASTER,UP,LOWER_UP> mtu
1500 qdisc noqueue state UP group default qlen 1000
    link/ether 08:00:27:ca:c3:ff brd ff:ff:ff:ff:ff:ff
    inet 192.168.56.102/24 brd 192.168.56.255 scope
global noprefixroute bond0
        valid_lft forever preferred_lft forever
    inet 192.168.56.104/24 brd 192.168.56.255 scope
global secondary bond0:1
        valid_lft forever preferred_lft forever
    inet 192.168.56.105/24 brd 192.168.56.255 scope
global secondary bond0:2
```

```
        valid_lft forever preferred_lft forever
[root@rac02 ~]#
```

The command asmcmd lsdg allows to visualize the diskgroups

```
[oragrid@rac01 ~]$ asmcmd lsdg
State     Type    Rebal  Sector  Logical_Sector  Block
AU  Total_MB  Free_MB  Req_mir_free_MB  Usable_file_MB
Offline_disks  Voting_files  Name
MOUNTED  NORMAL  N          512              512   4096
4194304     59988    12384            19996            -
3806             0            N  MGMTDB/
MOUNTED  NORMAL  N          512              512   4096
4194304     59988    59072            19996
19538            0            Y  OCR_VOTING/
[oragrid@rac01 ~]$
```

Installation RDBMS

The installation must be done here under the identity of the user oracle. It is first important to modify the access rights to the directory /ora01/app/oracle which is pointed to by ORACLE_BASE and which due to the previous installation belongs to oragrid.

To do as root on each node

```
cd /ora01/app
chown oracle oracle
```

On rac01 connect oracle and create the following directory

```
mkdir -p /ora01/app/oracle/product/19/DB
```

Position yourself in this directory and decompress the zip file.

```
cd /ora01/app/oracle/product/19/DB
unzip /INSTALL/LINUX.X64_193000_db_home.zip
```

SSH Keys

As for the user oragrid, it is necessary to generate the SSH keys for the user oracle and this on each node. We use the same utility as for oragrid but under another tree :

```
cd
/ora01/app/oracle/product/19/DB/oui/prov/resources/scri
pts
./sshUserSetup.sh -user oracle -hosts "rac01 rac02" -
advanced -confirm -noPromptPassphrase
```

4 times the utility will ask for the oracle password (here oracle01).

Create the response file under $HOME -> db19c.rsp

```
oracle.install.responseFileVersion=/oracle/install/
rspfmt_dbinstall_response_schema_v19.0.0
oracle.install.option=INSTALL_DB_SWONLY
UNIX_GROUP_NAME=oinstall
INVENTORY_LOCATION=/ora01/app/oraInventory
ORACLE_HOME=/ora01/app/oracle/product/19/DB
ORACLE_BASE=/ora01/app/oracle
oracle.install.db.InstallEdition=EE
oracle.install.db.OSDBA_GROUP=dba
oracle.install.db.OSOPER_GROUP=oper
oracle.install.db.OSBACKUPDBA_GROUP=backupdba
```

```
oracle.install.db.OSDGDBA_GROUP=dgdba
oracle.install.db.OSKMDBA_GROUP=kmdba
oracle.install.db.OSRACDBA_GROUP=racdba
oracle.install.db.rootconfig.executeRootScript=false
oracle.install.db.CLUSTER_NODES=rac01,rac02
```

As for the Grid Infrastrucure, launch a check of the prerequisites

```
./runInstaller -silent -responseFile
/home/oracle/db19c.rsp -executePrereqs
```

If everything is correct launch the runInstaller

```
./runInstaller -silent -responseFile
/home/oracle/db19c.rsp -waitForCompletion
```

Once the installation is complete, launch the following shell as root on both servers

```
/ora01/app/oracle/product/19/DB/root.sh
```

Once the installation is complete as root on both servers, modify the rights of the directories under /ora01

```
find /ora01 -type d | xargs chmod g+w
```

Database

First create the different diskgroups, then the database itself. In order to facilitate handling, when connecting as an oragrid, configure the environment correctly by modifying the .bash_profile file.

RAC01 server, add the following lines in .bash_profile of user oragrid

```
export SQLPATH=$HOME/sql
export ORACLE_PATH=$SQLPATH
export ORAENV_ASK=NO
export ORACLE_SID=+ASM1
. oraenv
```

RAC02 server, add the following lines in .bash_profile of user oragrid

```
export SQLPATH=$HOME/sql
export ORACLE_PATH=$SQLPATH
export ORAENV_ASK=NO
export ORACLE_SID=+ASM2
. oraenv
```

On each of the nodes as oragrid, create the $HOME/sql directory

```
mkdir $HOME/sql
cd $HOME/sql
```

Inside this directory create a login.sql file with the following lines :

```
define _editor=vi
set sqlprompt '&_user.@&_connect_identifier. >'
set linesize 250
set pagesize 50
```

Once the binaries are in place, you must configure the various ASM diskgroups before installing the database.

Connect oragrid on rac01 and check the presence of the diskgroups configured during installation and the available ASM disks.

Diskgroups configured

```
asmcmd lsdg
State    Type    Rebal  Sector  Logical_Sector  Block
AU  Total_MB  Free_MB  Req_mir_free_MB  Usable_file_MB
Offline_disks  Voting_files  Name
MOUNTED  NORMAL  N        512              512    4096
4194304    307200   256824           102400
77212           0             N  MGMTDB/
MOUNTED  NORMAL  N        512              512    4096
4194304     61440    60524            20480
20022           0             Y  OCR_VOTING/
```

- MGMTDB : Database Cluster Health Monitor (run on one node only)
- OCR_VOTING : Voting Disk + OCR

Disks ASM affected

```
asmcmd lsdsk
Path
/dev/asm01
/dev/asm02
/dev/asm03
/dev/asm04
/dev/asm05
/dev/asm06
```

Disks ASM usabled

```
asmcmd lsdsk --candidate
Path
/dev/asm07
/dev/asm08
/dev/asm09
/dev/asm10
/dev/asm11
/dev/asm12
/dev/asm13
/dev/asm14
/dev/asm15
```

Create diskgroups

As user oragrid, connect to sqlplus in sysasm

```
create diskgroup data01 normal redundancy
disk '/dev/asm07','/dev/asm08','/dev/asm09'
attribute
'compatible.asm'='19.3','compatible.rdbms'='19.3','au_s
ize'='4M';

create diskgroup fra01 normal redundancy
disk '/dev/asm10','/dev/asm11','/dev/asm12'
attribute
'compatible.asm'='19.3','compatible.rdbms'='19.3','au_s
ize'='4M';
```

Start the news diskgroups on rac02

```
srvctl start diskgroup -diskgroup data01 -node rac02
srvctl start diskgroup -diskgroup fra01 -node rac02
```

The following shell command verifies that the diskgroups have started correctly

```
for i in  $(crsctl stat res -t | grep dg | cut -d'.' -
f2);do srvctl status diskgroup -diskgroup $i;done
Le groupe de disques DATA01 est en cours d'exécution
sur rac01,rac02
Le groupe de disques FRA01 est en cours d'exécution sur
rac01,rac02
Le groupe de disques MGMTDB est en cours d'exécution
sur rac01,rac02
Le groupe de disques OCR_VOTING est en cours
d'exécution sur rac01,rac02
```

Always via the asmcm command, display of diskgroups.

```
asmcmd lsdg
State    Type    Rebal  Sector  Logical_Sector  Block
AU  Total_MB  Free_MB  Req_mir_free_MB  Usable_file_MB
Offline_disks  Voting_files  Name
MOUNTED  NORMAL  N         512              512    4096
4194304    149988   143992             49996
46998             0              N  DATA01/
MOUNTED  NORMAL  N         512              512    4096
4194304    149988   149112             49996
```

```
49558                  0                N  FRA01/
MOUNTED  NORMAL  N           512              512    4096
4194304      59988    12384           19996              -
3806                   0                N  MGMTDB/
MOUNTED  NORMAL  N           512              512    4096
4194304      59988    59072           19996
19538                  0                Y  OCR_VOTING/
```

Create a database

Creation must be done by the user oracle. To facilitate creation, the following shell script, $HOME/createYODA.sh, is in place.

At the start of the script, a certain number of variables to customize according to the database to be created, here a database named YODA.

```bash
#######################################################
# Shell for create a database RAC 19c YODA on 2 nodes
# EJN : 18/03/2020
# Note : 2 files ( initYODA.ora et createYODA.sql )
write under /home/oracle/sql
# Call : createYODA.sh
#######################################################
#!/bin/bash
export ORACLE_BASE=/ora01/app/oracle
export ORACLE_HOME=/ora01/app/oracle/product/19/DB
export PATH=$ORACLE_HOME/bin:$PATH

export DEBUT=$(date +%s)
echo $(date)


# Change variables if necessary
export DB=YODA
export DBUNIQ=${DB} # For dataguard configuration make
this different.
export DATA=DATA01
export FRA=FRA01
export INSTANCE1=${DBUNIQ}1
export INSTANCE2=${DBUNIQ}2
export SGA=1280M
export PGA=320M
export REDOSIZE=50M
# Character set is most important !!! Beware !!!
# WE8ISO8859P15 character coding on 1 byte
```

```
# AL32UTF8 character coding on 4 bytes
# export CHARACTERSET=WE8IS08859P15
export CHARACTERSET=AL32UTF8
# Never use @ in password, in production make password
more strong !!!
export MDP=Manager19#
export SERVER1=rac01
export SERVER2=rac02
export SRV1=YODA_APS
export SRV2=YODA_BAS1
export SRV3=YODA_BAS2


echo "Start create RAC database ${DBUNIQ} on 2 nodes
( ${SERVER1} - ${SERVER2} )"

# Record to Grid Infractructure
srvctl add database -database ${DBUNIQ} -pwfile +$
{DATA}/${DBUNIQ}/orapw${DBUNIQ} -oraclehome $
{ORACLE_HOME} -dbname ${DB}
srvctl add instance -database ${DBUNIQ} -instance
$INSTANCE1 -node ${SERVER1}
srvctl add instance -database ${DBUNIQ} -instance
$INSTANCE2 -node ${SERVER2}
srvctl setenv database -database ${DBUNIQ} -t
ORACLE_BASE=${ORACLE_BASE}
srvctl disable database -database ${DBUNIQ}


echo "Database ${DBUNIQ} record on GRID"
srvctl config database -database ${DBUNIQ}

# Directory for files init and create
if [ ! -d /home/oracle/sql ]
then
 mkdir -p /home/oracle/sql
fi


# File init.ora.
cat <<EOF > /home/oracle/sql/init${DB}.ora
*.audit_syslog_level='LOCAL1.WARNING'
*.audit_trail='DB','EXTENDED'
*.control_file_record_keep_time=35
*.db_name=${DB}
*.db_unique_name=${DBUNIQ}
*.db_block_size=8192
```

```
*.db_create_file_dest=+${DATA}
*.db_recovery_file_dest=+${FRA}
*.db_recovery_file_dest_size=100G
*.open_cursors=300
*.processes=300
*.log_archive_format=${DB}_%t_%s_%r.arch
*.sga_target=${SGA}
*.pga_aggregate_target=${PGA}
${INSTANCE1}.instance_number=1
${INSTANCE2}.instance_number=2
${INSTANCE1}.thread=1
${INSTANCE2}.thread=2
${INSTANCE1}.undo_tablespace=UNDOTBS1
${INSTANCE2}.undo_tablespace=UNDOTBS2
*.remote_login_passwordfile=exclusive
EOF

# Generate a ahell script for create
cat <<EOF > /home/oracle/sql/create${DB}.sql
create database ${DB}
character set ${CHARACTERSET}
national character set AL16UTF16
datafile size 500M autoextend on next 500M maxsize 5G
extent management local
sysaux datafile size 500M autoextend on next 500M
maxsize unlimited
undo tablespace UNDOTBS1 datafile size 500M  autoextend
on next 500M maxsize unlimited
default temporary tablespace TEMP tempfile size 500M
autoextend on next 500M maxsize unlimited
default tablespace DEFTBS datafile size 100K
logfile group 1 size ${REDOSIZE},
        group 2 size ${REDOSIZE},
        group 3 size ${REDOSIZE}
user sys identified by "${MDP}"
user system identified by "${MDP}";
EOF

# Creation of database
echo "Create instance and standards datafiles"
export ORACLE_SID=${DBUNIQ}
result=`sqlplus -s "/ as sysdba" <<EOF
startup nomount pfile=/home/oracle/sql/init${DB}.ora;
start /home/oracle/sql/create${DB}.sql;
```

```
exit;
EOF`

# Retreive names of control files
result=`sqlplus -s "/ as sysdba" <<EOF
set echo off
set feedback off
set pages 0
set linesize 2000
set heading off
select concat('*.control_files=''',
concat(replace(value, ', ', ''','''), '''')) ctl_files
from v\\$parameter where name ='control_files';
exit
EOF`
echo $result >> /home/oracle/sql/init${DB}.ora

echo "Database ${DBUNIQ} create. Control Files are in
place."
echo $result

# Password file
orapwd file=+${DATA}/${DBUNIQ}/orapw${DBUNIQ} force=y
format=12 dbuniquename=${DBUNIQ} password=${MDP}

echo "View of dictionary. Be patient !!!"
result=`sqlplus -s "/ as sysdba" <<EOF
create undo tablespace UNDOTBS2 datafile size 500M
autoextend on next 500M maxsize unlimited;

@?/rdbms/admin/catalog.sql
@?/rdbms/admin/catproc.sql
@?/rdbms/admin/catoctk.sql
@?/rdbms/admin/owminst.plb
@?/rdbms/admin/catclust.sql

grant sysdg to sysdg;
grant sysbackup to sysbackup;
grant syskm to syskm;
alter user dbsnmp identified by ${MDP} account unlock;

BEGIN
 FOR item IN ( SELECT USERNAME FROM DBA_USERS WHERE
ACCOUNT_STATUS IN ('OPEN', 'LOCKED', 'EXPIRED') AND
```

```
USERNAME NOT IN (
'SYS','SYSTEM','DBSNMP') )
 LOOP
   dbms_output.put_line('Locking and Expiring: ' ||
item.USERNAME);
   execute immediate 'alter user ' ||
          sys.dbms_assert.enquote_name(
          sys.dbms_assert.schema_name(
          item.USERNAME),false) || ' password expire
account lock' ;
 END LOOP;
END;
/

shutdown immediate;
startup mount pfile=/home/oracle/sql/init${DB}.ora
alter database open;
alter database add logfile thread 2 size ${REDOSIZE};
alter database add logfile thread 2 size ${REDOSIZE};
alter database add logfile thread 2 size ${REDOSIZE};
alter database enable public thread 2;

host echo "*.cluster_database=true" >>
/home/oracle/sql/init${DB}.ora
create spfile='+${DATA}/${DBUNIQ}/spfile${DB}' from
pfile='/home/oracle/sql/init${DB}.ora';

connect system/${MDP}
@?/sqlplus/admin/pupbld.sql
exit;
EOF`

result=`sqlplus -s "/ as sysdba" <<EOF
shutdown immediate;
exit;
EOF`

# Finalize
# Activate spfile by instance

echo "Finalize and integrate on GRID"
srvctl modify database -database ${DBUNIQ} -spfile "+$
{DATA}/${DBUNIQ}/spfile${DB}" -diskgroup "${DATA},$
{FRA}"
```

```
echo "SPFILE='+${DATA}/${DBUNIQ}/spfile${DB}'" >
$ORACLE_HOME/dbs/init${INSTANCE1}.ora
scp -q  $ORACLE_HOME/dbs/init${INSTANCE1}.ora $
{SERVEUR2}:$ORACLE_HOME/dbs/init${INSTANCE2}.ora

# Activate database by GRID
srvctl enable database -database ${DBUNIQ}
srvctl start database -database ${DBUNIQ}
srvctl status database -database ${DBUNIQ}

# Create services
srvctl add service -database ${DBUNIQ} -service ${SRV1}
-preferred ${INSTANCE1},${INSTANCE2}
srvctl add service -database ${DBUNIQ} -service ${SRV2}
-preferred ${INSTANCE1} -available ${INSTANCE2}
srvctl add service -database ${DBUNIQ} -service ${SRV3}
-preferred ${INSTANCE2} -available ${INSTANCE1}
srvctl start service -database ${DBUNIQ}

srvctl config database -database ${DBUNIQ}

export FIN=$(date +%s)
echo $(date)
export DUREE=$(( ${FIN} - ${DEBUT} ))
echo "End of create. Time -> ${DUREE}"
exit 0
```

Launch the shell

```
sh createYODA.sh
```

Post-installation

Add instances in /etc/oratab :

- YODA1   on   rac01   ->
  YODA1:/ora01/app/oracle/product/19/DB:N
- YODA2   on   rac02   ->
  YODA2:/ora01/app/oracle/product/19/DB:N

In Oracle connection, then create the $HOME/sql directory. This directory will contain the sql scripts that can be launched from SQL * Plus without specifying the location (SQLPATH environment variable).

```
mkdir -p $HOME/sql
```

In this directory is also located the login.sql file, which is read each time SQL * Plus is launched, and which allows configuration of the SQL * Plus environment. Create this file and add the following lines to it:

```
define _editor=vi
set sqlprompt '&_user.@&_connect_identifier. >'
set linesize 250
set pagesize 50
```

So under SQL * Plus when calling the editor vi will be launched in place of ed. The prompt is redefined in order to display the current Oracle*Net user and alias during the SQL*Plus session.

Alias

The installation at the start of the rlwrap package provides a reminder of the commands in the various oracle utilities.

User oragrid, .bashrc file, add the following lines on each node

```
alias sqlplus='rlwrap sqlplus'
alias asmcmd='rlwrap asmcmd'
alias adrci='rlwrap adrci'
```

User oracle, .bashrc file, add the following lines on each node

```
alias sqlplus='rlwrap sqlplus'
alias rman='rlwrap rman'
alias adrci='rlwrap adrci'
```

Script oraset

Do connection root and under /usr/local/bin create script oraset (
source Darl Kuhn Pro Oracle Database 12c Administration)
:

```bash
#!/bin/bash
# Environment Oracle
# Source Darl Kuhn Pro Administratio Oracle 12c.
# Original script modify for RAC.
# Setup: 1. Put this file under /usr/local/bin
#        2. Add /usr/local/bin in $PATH
# Use  : batch : . oraset <SID>
#        menu  : . oraset
#========================================================

# File oratab is not at the same place if OS Linux or
Solaris.
if [ -f /etc/oratab ]; then # Linux
  OTAB=/etc/oratab
elif [ -f /var/opt/oracle/oratab ]; then # Solaris
  OTAB=/var/opt/oracle/oratab
else
    echo 'oratab file not found.'
    exit
fi
#
if [ -z $1 ]; then
  SIDLIST=$(egrep -v '^#|\*|\+|-' ${OTAB} | cut -f1 -
d:)
  echo "Choice environment ( No choice : Q )"
  # PS3 : Prompt when use command select in shell BASH.
  PS3='SID? '
  select sid in ${SIDLIST}; do
    if [ -n $sid ]; then
      HOLD_SID=$sid
      break
    fi
    if [ "$sid" = "q" || "$sid" = "Q" ]; then
      break
    fi
  done
else
  if egrep -v '^#|\*' ${OTAB} | grep -w
"${1}:">/dev/null; then
```

```
      HOLD_SID=$1
    else
      echo "SID: $1 not exist in $OTAB"
    fi
    shift
  fi
#
export ORACLE_SID=$HOLD_SID
export ORACLE_HOME=$(egrep -v '^#|\*|\+|-' $OTAB|grep -
w $ORACLE_SID:|cut -f2 -d:)
#export GRID_HOME=$(egrep -v '^#|\*' $OTAB|grep -w ASM
|cut -f2 -d:)
export ORACLE_BASE=${ORACLE_HOME%%/product*}
export ADR_BASE=$ORACLE_BASE/diag
export TNS_ADMIN=$GRID_HOME/network/admin
export PATH=$ORACLE_HOME/bin:$PATH
export LD_LIBRARY_PATH=$ORACLE_HOME/lib
export NLS_LANG=FRENCH_FRANCE.UTF8
export NLS_DATE_FORMAT='DD/MM/YYYY HH24:MI:SS'
export SQLPATH=$HOME/sql
export ORACLE_PATH=$SQLPATH
```

ADRCI

Since the 11g version of Oracle the traces under managed by ADR
(Automatic Diagnostic Repository). The following shell offer
usefuls functions, adrci_fct to position under /usr/local/bin

```
# Functions ADRCI usefull
# Go to directory of traces.
function trace {
  TRACE=$(adrci exec="show homes" | grep $ORACLE_SID)
  cd ${ORACLE_BASE}/${TRACE}/trace
}

# Option -d for dynamical view of alert.log
function alert {
  TRACE=$(adrci exec="show homes" | grep $ORACLE_SID)
  if [ "$1" = "-d" ]; then
    adrci exec="set home ${TRACE};show alert -tail -f"
  else
    adrci exec="set home ${TRACE};show alert"
  fi
}
```

```
# Option -a to see all problem on all adr home.
function problem {
  if [ "$1" = "-a" ]; then
    for i in $( adrci exec="show homes" | grep -v "ADR
Homes:" )
    do
      adrci exec="set home ${i};show problem"
    done
  else
    TRACE=$(adrci exec="show homes" | grep $ORACLE_SID)
    adrci exec="set home ${TRACE};show problem"
  fi
}

function adrci_show_control {
  for i in $( adrci exec="show homes" | grep
$ORACLE_SID )
  do
    echo "SHOW CONTROL ${i}:"
    adrci exec="set home ${i}; show control;"
  done
}

function adrci_set_control {
  export SHORT=168 # 1 semaine ( 7 jours )
  export LONG=720 # 1 mois ( 30 jours )
  for i in $( adrci exec="show homes" | grep
$ORACLE_SID )
  do
    echo "set control ${i}:"
    adrci exec="set home ${i}; set control \
(SHORTP_POLICY=${SHORT}, LONGP_POLICY=${LONG}\);"
  done
}

function adrci_purge_trace {
  export TEMPS=240 # 4 hours
  for i in $( adrci exec="show homes" | grep
$ORACLE_SID )
  do
    adrci exec="set home ${i}; purge -age ${TEMPS}"
  done
}
```

If issue on adrci -> error : No ADR base is set. This is due to corruption or absence of the file /ora01/app/oracle/product/19/DB/log/diag/adrci_dir. This file contains the path to ORACLE_BASE. Under root connection create the following directory:

```
mkdir -p /ora01/app/oracle/product/19/DB/log/diag
chown -R oracle:oinstall
/ora01/app/oracle/product/19/DB/log
```

Under oracle connection generate this file.

```
printf "%s" "/ora01/app/oracle" >
/ora01/app/oracle/product/19/DB/log/diag/adrci_dir.mif
```

Add the following lines to user oracle .bash_profile on each node.

```
source /usr/local/bin/adrci_fct
source /usr/local/bin/oraset
```

Also add the following line to the user oragrid .bash_profile file on each node.

```
source /usr/local/bin/adrci_fct
```

HugePages

You must install the prerequisite package bc on the 2 nodes.

```
yum -y install bc
```

The /usr/local/bin/hugepages_settings.sh script. This script must be launched on both nodes, as user root) and take the highest value (the MGMTDB database only run on 1 node).

```
#!/bin/bash
#
# hugepages_settings.sh
#
# Linux bash script to compute values for the
# recommended HugePages/HugeTLB configuration
#
# Note: This script does calculation for all shared
memory
# segments available when the script is run, no matter
it
# is an Oracle RDBMS shared memory segment or not.
# Check for the kernel version
KERN=`uname -r | awk -F. '{ printf("%d.%d\n",
```

63

```
$1,$2); }'`
# Find out the HugePage size
HPG_SZ=`grep Hugepagesize /proc/meminfo | awk {'print
$2'}`
# Start from 1 pages to be on the safe side and
guarantee 1 free HugePage
NUM_PG=1
# Cumulative number of pages required to handle the
running shared memory segments
for SEG_BYTES in `ipcs -m | awk {'print $5'} | grep
"[0-9][0-9]*"`
do
    MIN_PG=`echo "$SEG_BYTES/($HPG_SZ*1024)" | bc -q`
    if [ $MIN_PG -gt 0 ]; then
        NUM_PG=`echo "$NUM_PG+$MIN_PG+1" | bc -q`
    fi
done
# Finish with results
case $KERN in
    '2.4') HUGETLB_POOL=`echo "$NUM_PG*$HPG_SZ/1024" |
bc -q`;
            echo "Recommended setting: vm.hugetlb_pool =
$HUGETLB_POOL" ;;
    '2.6' | '3.8' | '3.10' | '4.1' ) echo "Recommended
setting: vm.nr_hugepages = $NUM_PG" ;;
    *) echo "Unrecognized kernel version $KERN.
Exiting." ;;
esac
# End
```

As root edit the file /etc/sysctl.conf and add the line returned by the script, below an example.

```
vm.nr_hugepages = 1800
```

It is advised to put a see two pages more than the value returned by the script. Add also the following parameter:

```
vm.hugetlb_shm_group = 1002
```

This is the GID of the dba group. This parameter defines the security associated with HugePages. Only users who are part of the group whose gid is associated with this parameter can use them. Imperative on a RAC cluster.

Then activate with the command sysctl -p.

 HugesPages is not compatible with parameter MEMORY_TARGET.

To fully activate hugespages in Oracle, connect to sysdba and change the use_large_pages parameter (default to none).

```
alter system set use_large_pages=only sid='*'
scope=spfile;
```

By consulting the alert.log file of the database, we should see the use of the Huges Pages.

```
...
********************************************************
**************
Dump of system resources acquired for SHARED GLOBAL
AREA (SGA)
 Per process system memlock (soft) limit = UNLIMITED
 Expected per process system memlock (soft) limit to
lock
 instance MAX SHARED GLOBAL AREA (SGA) into memory:
1284M
 Available system pagesizes:
  4K, 2048K
 Supported system pagesize(s):
  PAGESIZE  AVAILABLE_PAGES  EXPECTED_PAGES
ALLOCATED_PAGES  ERROR(s)
     2048K           1800            642
642       NONE
 Reason for not supporting certain system pagesizes:
  4K - Large pagesizes only
********************************************************
**************
...
```

PSU

The establishment of the PSU will be described here at the time of writing, that of January 2020.

The PSUs are broadcast 4 times a year, generally on the 15th of the following months:

- january
- april
- july
- october

Oracle recommends applying them systematically.

Important : To apply PSU you must have an account on My Oracle Support, so you must buy a licence !!!!

Last version of opatch

Update the opatch program. To do on each node and each user (oracle and oragrid). The opatch zip file (p6880880_190000_Linux-x86-64.zip) is under / INSTALL on each server.

Connection oragrid

```
cd /ora01/app/oragrid/product/19/GI
rm -rf OPatch
unzip -q /INSTALL/p6880880_190000_Linux-x86-64.zip
```

Connection oracle

```
cd /ora01/app/oracle/product/19/DB
rm -rf OPatch
unzip -q /INSTALL/p6880880_190000_Linux-x86-64.zip
```

Apply PSU 01/2020

The PSU is delivered in the form of a zip file (p30501910_190000_Linux-x86-64.zip) which is present on each server in the / INSTALL directory. Unzip this file and give the correct rights. To do on the 2 nodes.

```
cd /INSTALL
unzip -q p30501910_190000_Linux-x86-64.zip
chown -R oragrid:oinstall 30501910
```

This PSU changes the basic version 19.3 to version 19.6.

Apply PSU on the first node

The advantage of a cluster is to be able to apply the PSUs without stopping the activity on the base. The action is done node by node.

 During the tests, the passage of this PSU generated some issues on the second node. These different points are seen during installation on the second node. All issues can be resolv with affect the correct rights on files or directories.

First pass the PSU on the first node, ie rac01. The launch of the PSU must be done under the root account. First, the analyze option allows you to test that everything is correct for the application of the PSU.

```
/ora01/app/oragrid/product/19/GI/OPatch/opatchauto
apply /INSTALL/30501910/ -analyze
```

If the analysis command is successful, launch the PSU application

```
/ora01/app/oragrid/product/19/GI/OPatch/opatchauto
apply /INSTALL/30501910/
```

Below the traces generated on the first node.

```
[root@rac01 ~]#
/ora01/app/oragrid/product/19/GI/OPatch/opatchauto
apply /INSTALL/30501910/

OPatchauto session is initiated at Sat Mar 28 08:06:22
2020

System initialization log file is
/ora01/app/oragrid/product/19/GI/cfgtoollogs/opatchauto
db/systemconfig2020-03-28_08-06-32AM.log.

Le fichier journal de session est
/ora01/app/oragrid/product/19/GI/cfgtoollogs/opatchauto
/opatchauto2020-03-28_08-07-48AM.log
```

L'ID de cette session est CXD8

Executing OPatch prereq operations to verify patch
applicability on home /ora01/app/oragrid/product/19/GI

Executing OPatch prereq operations to verify patch
applicability on home /ora01/app/oracle/product/19/DB
Patch applicability verified successfully on home
/ora01/app/oracle/product/19/DB

Patch applicability verified successfully on home
/ora01/app/oragrid/product/19/GI

Verifying SQL patch applicability on home
/ora01/app/oracle/product/19/DB
"/bin/sh -c 'cd /ora01/app/oracle/product/19/DB;
ORACLE_HOME=/ora01/app/oracle/product/19/DB
ORACLE_SID=YODA1
/ora01/app/oracle/product/19/DB/OPatch/datapatch -
prereq -verbose'" command failed with errors. Please
refer to logs for more details. SQL changes, if any,
can be analyzed by manually retrying the same command.

SQL patch applicability verified successfully on home /
ora01/app/oracle/product/19/DB

Preparing to bring down database service on home
/ora01/app/oracle/product/19/DB
Successfully prepared home
/ora01/app/oracle/product/19/DB to bring down database
service

Bringing down CRS service on home
/ora01/app/oragrid/product/19/GI
CRS service brought down successfully on home
/ora01/app/oragrid/product/19/GI

Performing prepatch operation on home
/ora01/app/oracle/product/19/DB
Perpatch operation completed successfully on home

68

/ora01/app/oracle/product/19/DB

Start applying binary patch on home
/ora01/app/oracle/product/19/DB
Binary patch applied successfully on home
/ora01/app/oracle/product/19/DB

Performing postpatch operation on home
/ora01/app/oracle/product/19/DB
Postpatch operation completed successfully on home
/ora01/app/oracle/product/19/DB

Start applying binary patch on home /ora01/app/oragrid/
product/19/GI
Binary patch applied successfully on home
/ora01/app/oragrid/product/19/GI

Starting CRS service on home
/ora01/app/oragrid/product/19/GI
CRS service started successfully on home
/ora01/app/oragrid/product/19/GI

Preparing home /ora01/app/oracle/product/19/DB after
database service restarted
No step execution required........

Trying to apply SQL patch on home
/ora01/app/oracle/product/19/DB
"/bin/sh -c 'cd
/ora01/app/oracle/product/19/DB;ORACLE_HOME=/ora01/app/
oracle/product/19/DB ORACLE_SID=YODA1
/ora01/app/oracle/product/19/DB/OPatch/datapatch -
verbose'" command failed with errors. Please refer to
logs for more details. SQL changes, if any, can be
applied by manually retrying the same command.

SQL patch applied successfully on home
/ora01/app/oracle/product/19/DB

```
OPatchAuto exécuté.

---------------------------------
Summary--------------------------------

Patching is completed successfully. Please find the
summary as follows:

Host:rac01
RAC Home:/ora01/app/oracle/product/19/DB
Version:19.0.0.0.0
Summary:

==Following patches were SKIPPED:

Patch: /INSTALL/30501910/30489632
Reason: This patch is not applicable to this specified
target type - "rac_database"

Patch: /INSTALL/30501910/30655595
Reason: This patch is not applicable to this specified
target type - "rac_database"


==Following patches were SUCCESSFULLY applied:

Patch: /INSTALL/30501910/30489227
Log:
/ora01/app/oracle/product/19/DB/cfgtoollogs/opatchauto/
core/opatch/opatch2020-03-28_08-12-27AM_1.log

Patch: /INSTALL/30501910/30557433
Log:
/ora01/app/oracle/product/19/DB/cfgtoollogs/opatchauto/
core/opatch/opatch2020-03-28_08-12-27AM_1.log


Host:rac01
CRS Home:/ora01/app/oragrid/product/19/GI
Version:19.0.0.0.0
Summary:

==Following patches were SUCCESSFULLY applied:
```

```
Patch: /INSTALL/30501910/30489227
Log:
/ora01/app/oragrid/product/19/GI/cfgtoollogs/opatchauto
/core/opatch/opatch2020-03-28_08-22-13AM_1.log

Patch: /INSTALL/30501910/30489632
Log:
/ora01/app/oragrid/product/19/GI/cfgtoollogs/opatchauto
/core/opatch/opatch2020-03-28_08-22-13AM_1.log

Patch: /INSTALL/30501910/30557433
Log:
/ora01/app/oragrid/product/19/GI/cfgtoollogs/opatchauto
/core/opatch/opatch2020-03-28_08-22-13AM_1.log

Patch: /INSTALL/30501910/30655595
Log:
/ora01/app/oragrid/product/19/GI/cfgtoollogs/opatchauto
/core/opatch/opatch2020-03-28_08-22-13AM_1.log

OPatchauto session completed at Sat Mar 28 08:39:25
2020
Time taken to complete the session 33 minutes, 4
seconds
```

We notice in these traces an error on the datapatch command.

```
...
Verifying SQL patch applicability on home
/ora01/app/oracle/product/19/DB
"/bin/sh -c 'cd /ora01/app/oracle/product/19/DB;
ORACLE_HOME=/ora01/app/oracle/product/19/DB
ORACLE_SID=YODA1
/ora01/app/oracle/product/19/DB/OPatch/datapatch -
prereq -verbose'" command failed with errors. Please
refer to logs for more details. SQL changes, if any,
can be analyzed by manually retrying the same command.
...
```

This command is used to update the data dictionary tables for each database. Do not take it into account and at the end of PSU it is possible to pass it manually (see below).

 The PSU on the first node goes without difficulty. On the second node many failures are due to rights problem.

Apply on the second node

The passage of this PSU on the second node seems quite laborious. In this paragraph various situations are presented. The command is identical, however there will probably be one or more failures, most of the time it is a problem of rights on files or directories. Below the trace.

```
[root@rac02 ~]#
/ora01/app/oragrid/product/19/GI/OPatch/opatchauto
apply /INSTALL/30501910/

OPatchauto session is initiated at Sat Mar 28 09:57:18
2020

System initialization log file is
/ora01/app/oragrid/product/19/GI/cfgtoollogs/opatchauto
db/systemconfig2020-03-28_09-57-27AM.log.

Le fichier journal de session est
/ora01/app/oragrid/product/19/GI/cfgtoollogs/opatchauto
/opatchauto2020-03-28_09-58-10AM.log
L'ID de cette session est UEA3

Executing OPatch prereq operations to verify patch
applicability on home /ora01/app/oracle/product/19/DB

Executing OPatch prereq operations to verify patch
applicability on home /ora01/app/oragrid/product/19/GI
Patch applicability verified successfully on home
/ora01/app/oracle/product/19/DB

Patch applicability verified successfully on home
/ora01/app/oragrid/product/19/GI


Verifying SQL patch applicability on home
/ora01/app/oracle/product/19/DB
```

SQL patch applicability verified successfully on home /
ora01/app/oracle/product/19/DB

Preparing to bring down database service on home
/ora01/app/oracle/product/19/DB
Successfully prepared home
/ora01/app/oracle/product/19/DB to bring down database
service

Bringing down CRS service on home
/ora01/app/oragrid/product/19/GI
CRS service brought down successfully on home
/ora01/app/oragrid/product/19/GI

Performing prepatch operation on home
/ora01/app/oracle/product/19/DB
Perpatch operation completed successfully on home
/ora01/app/oracle/product/19/DB

Start applying binary patch on home
/ora01/app/oracle/product/19/DB
Binary patch applied successfully on home
/ora01/app/oracle/product/19/DB

Performing postpatch operation on home
/ora01/app/oracle/product/19/DB
Postpatch operation completed successfully on home
/ora01/app/oracle/product/19/DB

Start applying binary patch on home /ora01/app/oragrid/
product/19/GI
Failed while applying binary patches on home
/ora01/app/oragrid/product/19/GI

Echec de l'exécution de l'action d'application de
patches [OPatchAutoBinaryAction], consultez le journal
pour obtenir plus de détails. Echecs :
Patch Target : rac02->/ora01/app/oragrid/product/19/GI

```
Type[crs]
Details: [
--------------------------Patching
Failed-------------------------------
Command execution failed during patching in home:
/ora01/app/oragrid/product/19/GI, host: rac02.
Command failed:
/ora01/app/oragrid/product/19/GI/OPatch/opatchauto
apply /INSTALL/30501910/ -oh
/ora01/app/oragrid/product/19/GI -target_type cluster -
binary -invPtrLoc
/ora01/app/oragrid/product/19/GI/oraInst.loc -jre
/ora01/app/oragrid/product/19/GI/OPatch/jre -
persistresult
/ora01/app/oragrid/product/19/GI/opatchautocfg/db/sessi
oninfo/sessionresult_rac02_crs.ser -analyzedresult
/ora01/app/oragrid/product/19/GI/opatchautocfg/db/sessi
oninfo/sessionresult_analyze_rac02_crs.ser
Command failure output:
==Following patches FAILED in apply:

Patch: /INSTALL/30501910/30489227
Log:
/ora01/app/oragrid/product/19/GI/cfgtoollogs/opatchauto
/core/opatch/opatch2020-03-28_10-15-44AM_1.log
Reason: Failed during Patching:
oracle.opatch.opatchsdk.OPatchException: Echec de
ApplySession dans la phase de modification du
système... 'ApplySession::apply failed:
java.io.IOException:
oracle.sysman.oui.patch.PatchException:
java.io.FileNotFoundException: /ora01/app/oraInventory/
ContentsXML/oui-patch.xml (Permission non accordée)'

After fixing the cause of failure Run opatchauto resume

]
OPATCHAUTO-68061: Echec du moteur dorchestration.
OPATCHAUTO-68061: Echec du moteur d'orchestration avec
le code retour 1
OPATCHAUTO-68061: Pour plus de détails, consultez le
journal.
Echec d'OPatchAuto.
```

```
OPatchauto session completed at Sat Mar 28 10:18:07
2020
Time taken to complete the session 20 minutes, 50
seconds

 opatchauto failed with error code 42
```

We see a problem of rights on the file
/ora01/app/oraInventory/ContentsXML/oui-patch.xml. Indeed the
write rights are not activated on the group as shown by the
following command

```
[root@rac02 ~]# ll /ora01/app/oraInventory/ContentsXML/
oui-patch.xml
-rw-r--r-- 1 oracle oinstall 174 28 mars  10:14 /ora01/
app/oraInventory/ContentsXML/oui-patch.xml
```

This problem did not occur on the first node where the rights are
correct as shown in the following command:

```
[root@rac01 ~]# ll /ora01/app/oraInventory/ContentsXML/
oui-patch.xml
-rw-rw---- 1 oragrid oinstall 174 28 mars  08:33
/ora01/app/oraInventory/ContentsXML/oui-patch.xml
[root@rac01 ~]#
```

We also notice that the owner is different: oragrid on rac01 and
oracle on rac02. We must not reason to use it but in a group
(oinstall). Simply modify the rights on this file and relaunch
opatchauto via the resume option

```
[root@rac02 ~]# chmod 0664
/ora01/app/oraInventory/ContentsXML/oui-patch.xml
[root@rac02 ~]#
/ora01/app/oragrid/product/19/GI/OPatch/opatchauto
resume
```

Below the generated trace

```
OPatchauto session is initiated at Sat Mar 28 10:21:29
2020
Le fichier journal de session est
/ora01/app/oragrid/product/19/GI/cfgtoollogs/opatchauto
/opatchauto2020-03-28_10-21-30AM.log
Reprise de la session existante avec l'ID UEA3

Start applying binary patch on home /ora01/app/oragrid/
```

```
product/19/GI

Binary patch applied successfully on home
/ora01/app/oragrid/product/19/GI

Checking shared status of home.....

Starting CRS service on home
/ora01/app/oragrid/product/19/GI
Failed to start CRS service on home /ora01/app/oragrid/
product/19/GI

Echec de l'exécution de l'action d'application de
patches [GIStartupAction], consultez le journal pour
obtenir plus de détails. Echecs :
Patch Target : rac02->/ora01/app/oragrid/product/19/GI
Type[crs]
Details: [
--------------------------Patching
Failed--------------------------------
Command execution failed during patching in home:
/ora01/app/oragrid/product/19/GI, host: rac02.
Command failed:  /ora01/app/oragrid/product/19/GI/perl/
bin/perl -I/ora01/app/oragrid/product/19/GI/perl/lib -
I/ora01/app/oragrid/product/19/GI/opatchautocfg/db/dbtm
p/bootstrap_rac02/patchwork/crs/install
-I/ora01/app/oragrid/product/19/GI/opatchautocfg/db/dbt
mp/bootstrap_rac02/patchwork/xag
/ora01/app/oragrid/product/19/GI/opatchautocfg/db/dbtmp
/bootstrap_rac02/patchwork/crs/install/rootcrs.pl -
postpatch
Command failure output:
Using configuration parameter file: /ora01/app/oragrid/
product/19/GI/opatchautocfg/db/dbtmp/bootstrap_rac02/
patchwork/crs/install/crsconfig_params
The log of current session can be found at:

/ora01/app/oracle/crsdata/rac02/crsconfig/crs_postpatch
_rac02_2020-03-28_10-34-28AM.log
2020/03/28 10:35:01 CLSRSC-329: Replacing Clusterware
entries in file 'oracle-ohasd.service'
Oracle Clusterware active version on the cluster is
[19.0.0.0.0]. The cluster upgrade state is [NORMAL].
The cluster active patch level is [2701864972].
```

```
SQL Patching tool version 19.6.0.0.0 Production on Sat
Mar 28 10:40:43 2020
Copyright (c) 2012, 2019, Oracle.  All rights reserved.

Error: prereq checks failed!
Could not create invocation log directory
/ora01/app/oracle/cfgtoollogs/sqlpatch/sqlpatch_17582_2
020_03_28_10_40_43: mkdir
/ora01/app/oracle/cfgtoollogs/sqlpatch/sqlpatch_17582_2
020_03_28_10_40_43: Permission denied at
/ora01/app/oragrid/product/19/GI/sqlpatch/sqlpatch.pm
line 947.

Please refer to MOS Note 1609718.1
for information on how to resolve the above errors.

SQL Patching tool complete on Sat Mar 28 10:40:43 2020
2020/03/28 10:40:43 CLSRSC-488: Patching the Grid
Infrastructure Management Repository database failed.

After fixing the cause of failure Run opatchauto resume

]
OPATCHAUTO-68061: Echec du moteur dorchestration.
OPATCHAUTO-68061: Echec du moteur d'orchestration avec
le code retour 1
OPATCHAUTO-68061: Pour plus de détails, consultez le
journal.
Echec d'OPatchAuto.

OPatchauto session completed at Sat Mar 28 10:40:47
2020
Time taken to complete the session 19 minutes, 19
seconds

 opatchauto failed with error code 42
```

Once again, there is a creation error due to a rights problem. By placing the following command, activate the write rights on the directories to the oinstall group and relaunch opatchauto resume.

```
[root@rac02 ~]# find /ora01 -type d | xargs chmod g+w
[root@rac02 ~]#
/ora01/app/oragrid/product/19/GI/OPatch/opatchauto
resume
```

Below the generated trace.

```
OPatchauto session is initiated at Sat Mar 28 10:42:17
2020
Le fichier journal de session est
/ora01/app/oragrid/product/19/GI/cfgtoollogs/opatchauto
/opatchauto2020-03-28_10-42-18AM.log
Reprise de la session existante avec l'ID UEA3

Starting CRS service on home
/ora01/app/oragrid/product/19/GI
Failed to start CRS service on home /ora01/app/oragrid/
product/19/GI

Echec de l'exécution de l'action d'application de
patches [GIStartupAction], consultez le journal pour
obtenir plus de détails. Echecs :
Patch Target : rac02->/ora01/app/oragrid/product/19/GI
Type[crs]
Details: [
--------------------------Patching
Failed-------------------------------
Command execution failed during patching in home:
/ora01/app/oragrid/product/19/GI, host: rac02.
Command failed:   /ora01/app/oragrid/product/19/GI/perl/
bin/perl -I/ora01/app/oragrid/product/19/GI/perl/lib -
I/ora01/app/oragrid/product/19/GI/opatchautocfg/db/dbtm
p/bootstrap_rac02/patchwork/crs/install
-I/ora01/app/oragrid/product/19/GI/opatchautocfg/db/dbt
mp/bootstrap_rac02/patchwork/xag
/ora01/app/oragrid/product/19/GI/opatchautocfg/db/dbtmp
/bootstrap_rac02/patchwork/crs/install/rootcrs.pl -
postpatch
Command failure output:
Using configuration parameter file: /ora01/app/oragrid/
product/19/GI/opatchautocfg/db/dbtmp/bootstrap_rac02/
patchwork/crs/install/crsconfig_params
The log of current session can be found at:

/ora01/app/oracle/crsdata/rac02/crsconfig/crs_postpatch
_rac02_2020-03-28_10-42-38AM.log
Oracle Clusterware active version on the cluster is
[19.0.0.0.0]. The cluster upgrade state is [NORMAL].
The cluster active patch level is [2701864972].
SQL Patching tool version 19.6.0.0.0 Production on Sat
```

```
Mar 28 10:49:43 2020
Copyright (c) 2012, 2019, Oracle.  All rights reserved.

Error: prereq checks failed!
Could not open sqlpatch history file /ora01/app/oracle/
cfgtoollogs/sqlpatch/sqlpatch_history.txt for writing

Please refer to MOS Note 1609718.1 and/or the
invocation log
/ora01/app/oracle/cfgtoollogs/sqlpatch/sqlpatch_28364_2
020_03_28_10_49_43/sqlpatch_invocation.log
for information on how to resolve the above errors.

SQL Patching tool complete on Sat Mar 28 10:49:43 2020
2020/03/28 10:49:43 CLSRSC-488: Patching the Grid
Infrastructure Management Repository database failed.

After fixing the cause of failure Run opatchauto resume

]
OPATCHAUTO-68061: Echec du moteur dorchestration.
OPATCHAUTO-68061: Echec du moteur d'orchestration avec
le code retour 1
OPATCHAUTO-68061: Pour plus de détails, consultez le
journal.
Echec d'OPatchAuto.

OPatchauto session completed at Sat Mar 28 10:49:47
2020
Time taken to complete the session 7 minutes, 31
seconds

 opatchauto failed with error code 42
```

A new error appears, again a problem of rights of writing on a file
at the level of the group.

```
[root@rac02 ~]# ll
/ora01/app/oracle/cfgtoollogs/sqlpatch/sqlpatch_history
.txt
-rw-r--r-- 1 oracle oinstall 113 28 mars  09:59 /ora01/
app/oracle/cfgtoollogs/sqlpatch/sqlpatch_history.txt
```

The following command allows the correction and restart again
opatchauto resume.

```
[root@rac02 ~]# chmod 0664
/ora01/app/oracle/cfgtoollogs/sqlpatch/sqlpatch_history
.txt
[root@rac02 ~]#
/ora01/app/oragrid/product/19/GI/OPatch/opatchauto
resume
```

Below the generated trace.

```
OPatchauto session is initiated at Sat Mar 28 10:51:12
2020
Le fichier journal de session est
/ora01/app/oragrid/product/19/GI/cfgtoollogs/opatchauto
/opatchauto2020-03-28_10-51-13AM.log
Reprise de la session existante avec l'ID UEA3

Starting CRS service on home
/ora01/app/oragrid/product/19/GI

CRS service started successfully on home
/ora01/app/oragrid/product/19/GI

Preparing home /ora01/app/oracle/product/19/DB after
database service restarted
Prepared home /ora01/app/oracle/product/19/DB
successfully after database service restarted

Trying to apply SQL patch on home
/ora01/app/oracle/product/19/DB

"/bin/sh -c 'cd
/ora01/app/oracle/product/19/DB;ORACLE_HOME=/ora01/app/
oracle/product/19/DB ORACLE_SID=YODA2
/ora01/app/oracle/product/19/DB/OPatch/datapatch -
verbose'" command failed with errors. Please refer to
logs for more details. SQL changes, if any, can be
applied by manually retrying the same command.

SQL patch applied successfully on home
/ora01/app/oracle/product/19/DB

OPatchAuto exécuté.

---------------------------------
Summary-----------------------------------
```

80

Patching is completed successfully. Please find the
summary as follows:

Host:rac02
RAC Home:/ora01/app/oracle/product/19/DB
Version:19.0.0.0.0
Summary:

==Following patches were SKIPPED:

Patch: /INSTALL/30501910/30489632
Reason: This patch is not applicable to this specified
target type - "rac_database"

Patch: /INSTALL/30501910/30655595
Reason: This patch is not applicable to this specified
target type - "rac_database"

==Following patches were SUCCESSFULLY applied:

Patch: /INSTALL/30501910/30489227
Log:
/ora01/app/oracle/product/19/DB/cfgtoollogs/opatchauto/
core/opatch/opatch2020-03-28_10-06-00AM_1.log

Patch: /INSTALL/30501910/30557433
Log:
/ora01/app/oracle/product/19/DB/cfgtoollogs/opatchauto/
core/opatch/opatch2020-03-28_10-06-00AM_1.log

Host:rac02
CRS Home:/ora01/app/oragrid/product/19/GI
Version:19.0.0.0.0
Summary:

==Following patches were SUCCESSFULLY applied:

Patch: /INSTALL/30501910/30489227
Log:
/ora01/app/oragrid/product/19/GI/cfgtoollogs/opatchauto
/core/opatch/opatch2020-03-28_10-21-57AM_1.log

```
Patch: /INSTALL/30501910/30489632
Log:
/ora01/app/oragrid/product/19/GI/cfgtoollogs/opatchauto
/core/opatch/opatch2020-03-28_10-21-57AM_1.log

Patch: /INSTALL/30501910/30557433
Log:
/ora01/app/oragrid/product/19/GI/cfgtoollogs/opatchauto
/core/opatch/opatch2020-03-28_10-21-57AM_1.log

Patch: /INSTALL/30501910/30655595
Log:
/ora01/app/oragrid/product/19/GI/cfgtoollogs/opatchauto
/core/opatch/opatch2020-03-28_10-21-57AM_1.log

OPatchauto session completed at Sat Mar 28 11:19:33
2020
Time taken to complete the session 28 minutes, 21
seconds
```

We notice again the datapatch error as on the node rac01. The easiest way is to start the command manually. Connect oracle and position on each base present. The action can be done from any node, here the choice of the node rac02 is voluntary in order to highlight the problem of rights which does not arise on the first node.

```
[oracle@rac02 ~]$ cd $ORACLE_HOME/OPatch/
[oracle@rac02 OPatch]$ ./datapatch -verbose
```

Below the generated trace.

```
SQL Patching tool version 19.6.0.0.0 Production on Sat
Mar 28 11:21:20 2020
Copyright (c) 2012, 2019, Oracle.  All rights reserved.

Log file for this invocation:
/ora01/app/oracle/cfgtoollogs/sqlpatch/sqlpatch_26700_2
020_03_28_11_21_20/sqlpatch_invocation.log

Connecting to database...OK
Gathering database info...done
Bootstrapping registry and package to current
versions...done
Determining current state...done
```

```
Current state of interim SQL patches:
  No interim patches found

Current state of release update SQL patches:
  Binary registry:
    19.6.0.0.0 Release_Update 191217155004: Installed
  SQL registry:
    Applied 19.6.0.0.0 Release_Update 191217155004 with
errors on 28/03/20 11:19:26,649056

Adding patches to installation queue and performing
prereq checks...done
Installation queue:
  No interim patches need to be rolled back
  Patch 30557433 (Database Release Update :
19.6.0.0.200114 (30557433)):
    Apply from 19.1.0.0.0 Feature Release to 19.6.0.0.0
Release_Update 191217155004
  No interim patches need to be applied

Installing patches...
Patch installation complete.  Total patches installed:
1

Validating logfiles...done
Patch 30557433 apply: WITH ERRORS
  logfile:
/ora01/app/oracle/cfgtoollogs/sqlpatch/30557433/2330530
5/30557433_apply_YODA_2020Mar28_11_22_11.log (errors)

Can't use string ("Could not open logfile
/ora01/ap"...) as a HASH ref while "strict refs" in use
at /ora01/app/oracle/product/19/DB/sqlpatch/sqlpatch.pm
line 6127.

Please refer to MOS Note 1609718.1 and/or the
invocation log
/ora01/app/oracle/cfgtoollogs/sqlpatch/sqlpatch_26700_2
020_03_28_11_21_20/sqlpatch_invocation.log
for information on how to resolve the above errors.

SQL Patching tool complete on Sat Mar 28 11:26:18 2020
```

This error is again a problem of rights. As root on the second node place the following command.

```
find /ora01 -type d | xargs chmod g+w
```

Reconnect oracle and relaunch datapatch.

```
[oracle@rac02 OPatch]$ ./datapatch -verbose
SQL Patching tool version 19.6.0.0.0 Production on Sat
Mar 28 11:31:20 2020
Copyright (c) 2012, 2019, Oracle.  All rights reserved.

Log file for this invocation:
/ora01/app/oracle/cfgtoollogs/sqlpatch/sqlpatch_32222_2
020_03_28_11_31_20/sqlpatch_invocation.log

Connecting to database...OK
Gathering database info...done
Bootstrapping registry and package to current
versions...done
Determining current state...done

Current state of interim SQL patches:
  No interim patches found

Current state of release update SQL patches:
  Binary registry:
    19.6.0.0.0 Release_Update 191217155004: Installed
  SQL registry:
    Applied 19.6.0.0.0 Release_Update 191217155004 with
errors on 28/03/20 11:26:17,367985

Adding patches to installation queue and performing
prereq checks...done
Installation queue:
  No interim patches need to be rolled back
  Patch 30557433 (Database Release Update :
19.6.0.0.200114 (30557433)):
    Apply from 19.1.0.0.0 Feature Release to 19.6.0.0.0
Release_Update 191217155004
  No interim patches need to be applied

Installing patches...
Patch installation complete.  Total patches installed:
1

Validating logfiles...done
Patch 30557433 apply: SUCCESS
```

```
   logfile:
/ora01/app/oracle/cfgtoollogs/sqlpatch/30557433/2330530
5/30557433_apply_YODA_2020Mar28_11_32_11.log (no
errors)
SQL Patching tool complete on Sat Mar 28 11:36:19 2020
[oracle@rac02 OPatch]$
```

By connecting to the database and querying the history, you can
view the two failures and on the third try the success.

```
SYS@YODA2 >set serverout on;
SYS@YODA2 >exec dbms_qopatch.get_sqlpatch_status;

Patch Id : 30557433
      Action : APPLY
      Action Time : 28-MARS -2020 11:19:26
      Description : Database Release Update :
19.6.0.0.200114 (30557433)
      Logfile : /ora01/app/oracle/cfgtoollogs/sqlpatch/
30557433/23305305/30557433_apply_YODA_2020Mar28_11_12_5
6.log
      Status : WITH ERRORS

Patch Id : 30557433
      Action : APPLY
      Action Time : 28-MARS -2020 11:26:17
      Description : Database Release Update :
19.6.0.0.200114 (30557433)
      Logfile : /ora01/app/oracle/cfgtoollogs/sqlpatch/
30557433/23305305/30557433_apply_YODA_2020Mar28_11_22_1
1.log
      Status : WITH ERRORS

Patch Id : 30557433
      Action : APPLY
      Action Time : 28-MARS -2020 11:36:16
      Description : Database Release Update :
19.6.0.0.200114 (30557433)
      Logfile : /ora01/app/oracle/cfgtoollogs/sqlpatch/
30557433/23305305/30557433_apply_YODA_2020Mar28_11_32_1
1.log
      Status : SUCCESS

Procédure PL/SQL terminée avec succès.
SYS@YODA2 >
```

By connecting either oracle or oragrid the opatch lspatches command allows you to check the installed patches.

Connection oracle

```
[oracle@rac02 ~]$ cd $ORACLE_HOME/OPatch
[oracle@rac02 OPatch]$ ./opatch lspatches
30557433;Database Release Update : 19.6.0.0.200114
(30557433)
30489227;OCW RELEASE UPDATE 19.6.0.0.0 (30489227)

OPatch succeeded.
```

It is possible by connecting sqlplus on the base to check the application of patches

```
SYS@YODA2 >select
xmltransform(dbms_qopatch.is_patch_installed('30557433'
),dbms_qopatch.get_opatch_xslt) "Patch installed?" from
dual;

Patch installed?
----------------
Patch Information:
      30557433:   applied on 2020-03-28T10:09:58+01:00

SYS@YODA2 >select
xmltransform(dbms_qopatch.is_patch_installed('30489227'
),dbms_qopatch.get_opatch_xslt) "Patch installed?" from
dual;

Patch installed?
----------------
Patch Information:
      30489227:   applied on 2020-03-28T10:06:38+01:00

SYS@YODA2 >
```

The following two SQL queries are also useful for viewing the application of patches.

```
select * from sys.registry$history;
select * from sys.dba_registry_sqlpatch;
```

Connection oragrid

```
[oragrid@rac02 ~]$ cd $ORACLE_HOME/OPatch
[oragrid@rac02 OPatch]$ ./opatch lspatches
30655595;TOMCAT RELEASE UPDATE 19.0.0.0.0 (30655595)
30557433;Database Release Update : 19.6.0.0.200114
(30557433)
30489632;ACFS RELEASE UPDATE 19.6.0.0.0 (30489632)
30489227;OCW RELEASE UPDATE 19.6.0.0.0 (30489227)

OPatch succeeded.
```

The opatch lsinventory command also gives a lot of information.

All of issue during apply PSU on the second node attributable to Oracle, which requires that the user oracle and oragrid have an umask equal to 0022. It would be more logical for the umask to be 0002.

Conclusion

This document is not a reference documentation for the construction of a RAC 19c cluster with
2 nodes, it is only the result of a personal experience based on installations made in clientele.
The transposition on VMs of a real infrastructure comprising physical servers, network switches
and SAN bay has for objective only pedagogy. To date, many 19c clusters with 2 nodes
installed in this way operate in production in 24 x 7 environments.

Any comments via the author's mailbox will be studied with pleasure.

Good reading.

Erik Jourdain